CROATOAN
Birthplace of America

By Scott Dawson

INFINITY
PUBLISHING

ISBN 0-7414-5469-6

Printed in the United States of America

Published June 2010

INFINITY PUBLISHING
1094 New DeHaven Street, Suite 100
West Conshohocken, PA 19428-2713
Toll-free (877) BUY BOOK
Local Phone (610) 941-9999
Fax (610) 941-9959
Info@buybooksontheweb.com
www.buybooksontheweb.com

I dedicate this book to my two girls,
Kirra Oceana Dawson and Sabra Flowers Dawson.

.

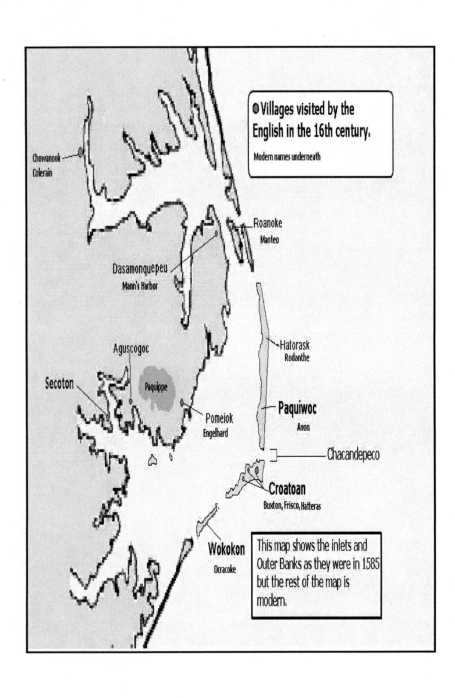

Chowanook
Colerain

● Villages visited by the
English in the 16th century.

Modern names underneath

Roanoke
Manteo

Dasamonquepeu
Mann's Harbor

Hatorask
Rodanthe

Aguscogoc

Secoton

Paquippe

Paquiwoc
Avon

Pomeiok
Engelhard

Chacandepeco

Croatoan
Buxton, Frisco, Hatteras

Wokokon
Ocracoke

This map shows the inlets and
Outer Banks as they were in 1585
but the rest of the map is
modern.

Table of Contents

Introduction

Y ou may have heard the tale of the Lost Colony. If so, you probably heard that 117 English colonists disappeared in 1587 and left no clues as to where they went and that nothing has ever been found to shed some light on the mystery.

This book is an attempt to educate the public about the Lost Colony of 1587, America's oldest mystery, and a story so wrapped in myth that many facts as to their whereabouts seem to have been ignored over the years. Recent archeological digs on Hatteras Island, together with genealogy, oral history, and the primary sources of the many voyages that took place from 1584 to 1590, give clues as to the whereabouts of the missing colony.

The first clue is a message carved on a palisade that was discovered by Governor John White in 1590 on Roanoke Island. The message said CROATOAN in capital letters. Before John White left the colony in 1587 to get supplies from England, he told the colonists to carve the name of the place they were going on a tree if they left Roanoke Island and to put a cross under it if they left for reasons of danger. No cross was found, and John in his own records stated he was relieved to know that the colony was safe in Croatoan with Manteo. Manteo was an Indian from Croatoan who had been to England twice, spoke English and had been used as an interpreter. John White had a daughter and granddaughter among the missing colonists and made an attempt to go to Croatoan to pick them up during his 1590 voyage, but he was turned back by foul weather that drowned seven of his company.

So where is Croatoan and were the English familiar with this place? Croatoan is modern day Buxton on Hatteras Island. Croatoan was an island the English had visited on all of their voyages. It was where they had originally landed in 1584 and even lived for a time in 1585. The Lost Colony went there again in 1587 and had a feast. It was the hometown of their ally and interpreter Manteo and appears on all of John White's maps. So yes, the English were familiar with Croatoan and there has never been a mystery as to where that place was.

However, after John White's failed attempt to reach the island in 1590, <u>no other attempt to reach Croatoan was made for another 114 years!</u> If anything, the fact that no one went back to Croatoan is a greater mystery than where the colony went. The next European to travel to Hatteras (on purpose and not by shipwreck) was John Lawson in 1701. Lawson published a book called *A New Voyage To Carolina* that is the definitive work on the North Carolina Indians of the 1700's. In this book, Lawson recorded that many of the Hatteras Indians or Croatoan had grey eyes and said that their ancestors could speak out of a book (read) and that they were indeed descendents of the 1587 colony. These Indians even said that a ship, which they called Sir Walter Raleigh's ship, still appeared among them. Lawson goes on to say that this tribe was very proud of their affinity to the English and some still wore English clothes.

So we have the message on the palisade, Manteo's home town, and the oral history of the Hatteras Indians all pointing to Croatoan. All of this is old news though. What is really interesting is what happened in 1993. The native families of Hatteras Island can show you arrowheads, pottery and other artifacts that they have found from what all who live there believe to be, the old Croatoan village site. In the 1970's, locals of the island used to sit by the road and sell arrowheads for a nickel each to tourists. Buckets full of pottery and arrowheads could be found all over the ridges where Croatoan Village once stood. In 1993, however,

Hurricane Emily surged 10 feet of sound tide over this village site and ripped out many layers of sand in the process. As a result, an enormous amount of new artifacts were uncovered and found by local residents, Zander Brody, Eddie Oaks, Keri Hooper and many others.

Eventually, archeologists came to the site. Dr. David Phelps had found some Croatoan artifacts before back in the 1980's while doing some work for the 400th anniversary of the first English voyages to the New World. Phelps returned to the island and with help from a lot of volunteers, struck pay dirt. This time not only were Croatoan artifacts found but European ones as well. Among the European artifacts were the iron ring of a caulking hammer, lead shot, nails, bricks and, most importantly, a gunlock that dates to 1583 and a gold insignia ring that probably belonged to a man named Master Kendall, who was part of the 1585 voyage. This ring and gunlock found by David Phelps now reside at East Carolina University. More and more artifacts come out of the Croatoan site each time they dig. Even European skeletons have been found along with Native American bones.

These finds led to a search of the genealogy of the old islander families along with deed records of the land where the artifacts were discovered. So far, this has been a great success. Due in part to the isolation of the island, many of the families have been living there for over 400 years and bear the surnames and genealogy to prove it. (This author's family being one of them). The Native American blood is obvious in the physical features of almost all the old families. The question now is not where did the colony go, but what happened after they reached Hatteras Island? There is some evidence to suggest that there was a break in the colony and that some of them moved inland while some remained on Hatteras Island. I will elaborate more on this later.

To understand the story of the Lost Colony, one must read and understand the voyages that preceded it. The problem for most people is that the primary sources are in Old English, incomplete, and vague at times on purpose due to the fact that the colony was a secret. The English were at war with Spain and if the location of their settlement got out, the Spanish would find and kill the colonists. The Spanish had already killed off a French attempt to settle down in Florida back in 1562, killing over 130 men. This massacre heavily shaped the mindset and preparations that went into the English voyages.

There are five 16th century voyages to the New World that will be covered in this book. The first is the 1584 recon mission, where Amadas and Barlowe are sent to find a good place for a future, larger settlement. They are looking for a place with three things: a good defensive position to protect against Spain, natural resources, and friendly native people. The next voyage is the one in 1585, which was a military settlement led by Ralph Lane and Richard Grenville that lasted almost a year and was very poorly managed. Then we have the 1586 resupply voyage where only 15 men are left to hold the fort. Finally, we have the Lost Colony of 1587, and last, John White's return to search for the colony in 1590.

To help tell the story, I have created a narrative history in modern English of the 16th century voyages and added some smells, sights and sounds to help the story come to life from the primary sources. At the end of each chapter are excerpts from the primary sources that the chapter was based on along with analysis of the facts. The last few chapters of this book deal with the recent discoveries and theories in a strictly factual manner. I hope to shed some light on America's greatest mystery and also entertain the reader.

It is important to remember that nowhere in the scholarly work is the colony of 1587 referred to as lost or missing until 1937. The concept or notion that the colony vanished without a trace was invented in 1937 to help sell tickets to what is now a famous outdoor drama. The mystery is nothing more than a marketing scheme and will be clearly demonstrated as such in this book. A close look at the primary sources reveals the rather obvious fact that the colony was never lost but abandoned at Croatoan. What is more important is the misrepresentation and insulting portrayal of the Native peoples that has been perpetuated as a result of the mythology created in 1937 that still holds strong today. My goal is simply to tell the truth. If that kills the mystery and hurts those who profiteer on lies... so be it.

Worlds Collide

~ July 4th 1584 ~

Captains Phillip Amadas and Arthur Barlowe and their crews arrive in the New World from England on two ships, the Admiral and the Roebuck. Their mission is to find a good place for a military settlement that will come later. In addition to finding a good defensive position to hold against Spain, they are to note the profitable resources of the area and test the temperament of the native people. They arrive and land at Croatoan. This is the first time the English have ever set foot on this continent, 23 years before Jamestown, and 36 years before the pilgrims at Plymouth Rock.

No words can describe the beauty of Croatoan. Only the eyes that have seen it first hand can grasp the majestic and awesome beauty of the place. It is here that two ocean currents meet and do constant battle. The warm clear waters of the Gulf Stream carry large schools of tuna, dolphin, and flying fish crashing headlong into the cold Labrador Current. The Labrador brings red drum, blue fish, and striper into the melee making two underwater worlds collide. The waves on even the calmest of days smash into each other heading opposite directions and shoot columns of white water into the air to be whipped around into spray by the ever present wind. This fight goes on in an unbroken line for over twelve miles perpendicular to the shore, depositing sand to form a great point that peels off at a right angle to form the Island of Croatoan itself. It is here at this chaotic stretch of sea that the English make their first contact with the New World.

The land is a maritime forest full of grapevines, green and yellow parrots, and large twisted live oaks covered in Spanish moss. Pelicans glide dangerously close to the surface of the sea picking out yellow bellied croaker. Ghost crabs and sand fleas scour in the wash, and white-tailed deer run across the flat forest bottoms to dine on blackberries and oats.

Opposite the seaside of the Island lay the Mentso (Pamlico Sound), mother to millions of oysters, blue claw crabs, and clams. The Sound is less than three feet deep for over a mile out and separates the island from the mainland at a distance of thirty-five miles. Croatoan is an isolated paradise for the local inhabitants, where they can live a life of harmony with the Earth.

Two young men, Tamoneok and Manteo, dressed in nothing but deerskins tied around the waist, drag sapling sticks along the beach searching for clams when they see them. Two ships are approaching. This is not the first time they have seen the "great canoes." The men drop their sticks. Manteo sprints to tell the village on the soundside of the island, located on a tiny wooded ridge about two miles away. Tamoneok scrambles up a live oak on the edge of the beach to keep an eye on the ships.

"Lord be praised, what a glorious land!" Barlowe says to a crowded quarterdeck as the men gaze at flocks of ducks, sea gulls and other fowl they have never seen before swarming around a white sandy beach leading up to a strip of lush green forest that stretches out of view. The sweet aroma of the pampas grasses and sea oats fill the men's nostrils, and the offshore breeze cools their faces from the sun. The sky is cloudless and dolphins are cutting through the waves between the ships and shore.

"Ready the boats and drop the anchors men. We are going ashore!" Amadas's voice was crisp and soldierly.

All of the men were happy to be going ashore. They thought they had reached the mainland and were eager to dine on the ducks and fish they could already see were in abundance. Hopes ran high of finding gold, silver, or other jewels.

As the men row to shore, they can see fish swimming all around them. The water is clear and the rising tide helps push them to shore. Upon reaching the beach, they notice green grapes rolling around in the wash and vines crawling up the sides of giant red cedar trees. The men jump out and plant an English flag in the sand. Amadas orders the men to unload the ships as he stands by the flag. The men all gather around him and listen as a short ceremony begins to claim the land for Queen Elizabeth and praises are made to God.

From a hilltop, Tamoneok watches the English. He is too far away to hear anything but too cautious to make any noise himself. The English were a source of curiosity, but the ship was a greater marvel. The only thing Tamoneok could compare it to was a twenty-six year old shipwreck whose remnants still poked out of the sand. Manteo came trotting back from the woods and told Tamoneok news from the village. The chief's brother, Granganimeo, asked for everyone to avoid the northeast end of the island where the strangers had landed. He then told Manteo to spy on the strangers with Tamoneok in order to get a good idea of their number and purpose. The chief is not on the island. He is nursing wounds in his legs on the mainland. Word is being sent to him by canoe of the strangers' presence.

Tamoneok whispers to Manteo in native tongue that he thinks the men look like turtles because the English are wearing great shells. He has never seen anyone in armor before and admires how the sun glistens off the silver "shells." The two Indians watch the English climb a hill, all the while easily shadowing their movements without detection. Manteo tells Tamoneok that the newcomers smell like turtles as well. Tamoneok stifles a laugh. Indeed the Englishmen had spent months in tight quarters without any bathing, and their stench announced their presence to any creature with nostrils.

A terrible noise like thunder suddenly rang out, shaking dozens of white cranes into the air and freezing the two Indians, gripping them with fear. Three more times the thunderous bark rang out. The English were shooting a harquebus over the Sound to see what animals it might stir up. Manteo and Tamoneok squat low behind the blackberry bushes with their hearts racing. They think about running to the village but elect to lie low.

"These cedars will make fine timbers for our shipyards back home, and I have already seen several deer tracks and rabbits. If nothing else, at least we shall eat well here," Amadas remarked to Barlowe.

Behind Amadas and Barlowe were John Wood and his brother Ben. John and Ben were alcoholic sailors pressed into service after one too many fist fights around the docks of Plymouth. Amadas had taught them some level of self-discipline through hard work, but the desire for a strong drink never wavered.

"I bet these ridges are full of gold, John. First thing I am going to buy once I am rich is me own tavern so's we can ave all the drinks we wants."

Back in the village called Croatoan, a meeting is being held inside the smoking lodge. It is decided that only one person should go and meet the newcomers. This way the visitors will not feel threatened. Later, Granganimeo and his servants will go and greet the 'turtle people' as they are being called. The elders remember the last time white faces had landed here and what a great benefit it was to the tribe. Metal rivets from a Spanish shipwreck of over twenty years ago are still being used to hollow out cypress trees to make canoes. Discussion of the prospect of more metal and other wonders fills the smoke lodge.

Tools, however, were not the only things left by the Spanish. One of the elders points out the entrance of the smoke lodge to two auburn haired girls playing outside. The others nod and agree they must be friendly but cautious. It is decided another day of observation without any contact should pass before anyone is permitted to talk to the English.

The English were busy roving around the forest re-cording the useful plants and resources. They had not seen any of the natives, but they had seen lots of footprints across ground that they themselves had not yet walked upon. Due to this discovery, they stayed near the ships and traveled in mass when in the woods. At night, they returned to the ships to sleep.

A celebration was held the first night on the weather deck. The men played lutes and stomped a tune. They were happy to have fresh grapes and had already begun the task of making wine from some of them. Fresh rabbit meat and blackberries were a pleasant change from the stale bread and salted pork they had sucked down for the past two months aboard the ships.

The night air was warm and the stars looked close enough to touch. The men were happy with what had been found already and still held fast to hopes of riches. Amadas wished to stay only long enough to lift his crew's spirits and health. He too was pleased with the island but desperately wanted to push further and find the mainland. The sailors watched comets and shooting stars as they listened to the roll of the waves. Their bellies were full, their faces a little sunburnt, and their hopes and dreams ran high as they drifted to sleep with smiles on their faces.

Back in the village, Manteo was informed that he had been chosen to greet the newcomers. The elders, including Manteo's mother, advised him not to take any weapons with him. He was to go alone and show only friendly smiles and gestures. Manteo agreed to go at dawn. The elders knew that they must not cause the "turtle people" any fear.

Manteo stayed up most of the night looking at the stars and praying to his ancestors. As he prayed, he watched the smoke from a nearby fire rise and curl, soon becoming the image of a bird's tail-feather dancing its way across an even surface. It left a smooth, curving black trail in its wake, the trail widening in the curves it took. Every so often the feather would skip once, sometimes twice in a row, breaking the trail.

Slowly, Manteo drifted asleep inside of his reed and sapling house with the images of the English replaying in his head. Their beards were a great source of curiosity but not half as much as their great canoes that came from the rising sun. Would they have wassador (metal) like the men before them? Were they in search of those men? What was it that shook the birds into the air and made the thunder clap?

In order not to disrupt the flow of the story, I have chosen to add direct quotes from Arthur Barlowe's report in italics here rather than throughout the text. I have left in the original spelling as well. Here are a few quotes from Barlowe himself that the chapter was based on:

"We passed from the Sea side towardes the toppes of those hilles next adjoyning, being but of meane higth and from thence wee behelde the Sea on both sides to the North, and to the South, finding no ende any of both wayes. This lande lay stretching it selfe to the West, which wee found to bee but an island of twentie miles long. (From modern day Buxton to Hatteras Inlet today is 20 miles). Under the banke or hill whereon we stoode, we behelde the valleys replenished with goodly cedar trees, and having discharged our harquebus-shot, such a flocke of Cranes (for the most part white) arose under us, with such a cry redoubled by many echoes, as if an armie of men had showted all together. This island had many goodly woodes full of deere, conies, hares, and fowle, even in the middest of summer in incredible abundance."

From Barlowe's report, we know they entered an inlet and took a left to an island that was 20 miles long running from East to West. We also know that the English could not see the mainland from this island. Later, Barlowe and 7 others left this island and headed North where *"wee came to an island called Raonoak,..."* Only 8 men of the entire company ever went to Roanoke Island in 1584. The rest of the men stayed on Hatteras Island where they had landed.

Barlowe mistakenly called the island he landed on winganicoa, which means: welcome friend when speaking to someone you are not related to. When addressing a relative each family member was greeted by a specific word. (see Croatoan word list at the back of the book.) It does not take much deduction to know Barlowe was on Hatteras/Croatoan. It is South of Roanoke, 20 miles long from East to West and you cannot see the mainland. Ocracoke also fits the description but Barlowe mentions standing on a hill large enough that cranes arose from underneath him. Hatteras Island has hills over 40 feet in elevation that run for miles covered with cedars, deer and rabbits just as Barlowe stated. Ocracoke's highest point is about 4 feet above sea level.

Deerskins and Swivel Guns

Manteo awoke before dawn and took his canoe to a point of land directly in front of where the ships were anchored. He began to pace up and down the point. His heart was pounding with anticipation and he was smiling as big as he could, just as the elders had suggested. In the woods beyond the beach, several of the villagers watched in silence, ready to come to Manteo's aid should he need it.

Aboard the Roebuck a loud voice cries out from the main bowl high up the mast.

"Sir… Master Barlowe! Look! There is a man out there! He is pacing back and forth!" John Wood startled the ship's crew with his news. John had been on watch while most were still asleep. Everyone was awake now and all eyes were on Manteo. They whisper to themselves, "It might be a trap."

Across thirty yards of water standing on the beach is a man wearing nothing but a deerskin with his hands on his hips smiling. The sun is just peeking over the horizon.

"Arm yourselves men, but do not fire a shot or strike a blow without orders. Six of you will accompany me ashore and see what this man wants. We will load up the falcon with grapeshot first and rake any war parties that should spring out of the woods. Do not attack without command. Perhaps he wants to trade, mayhap gold even." Amadas spoke like a soldier as he put on his helmet and headed for the longboat.

Manteo waited and held his smile. Here came a long-boat full of armed men straight for him. The English drug their longboat ashore and greeted this man.

"Hello," said Amadas with a smile and a raised hand. He was greeted by Manteo with a language he had never heard before, and a similar hand raise. No one knew what Manteo was saying but he pointed at the ships as he spoke. Manteo was asking them if they were looking for the men who had arrived in great canoes before. The English did not know what he was saying but guessed that he wanted to see the inside of the ships. They waved him on board the longboat and Manteo stepped on board with a smile and sat down and continued to talk. The English shook their heads and laughed as they remarked to each other what they supposed he was saying.

John Wood addressed the entire longboat, "I think he be saying, 'quick pass me a pair of breeches, me bullocks are freezing!'" A raucous laughter raised as the men threw their heads back. Manteo smiled nervously. The men rowed back to the ship and Manteo followed them on board.

The Admiral began to move and pulled up beside the Roebuck. A strange, dark, near-naked man was boarding and everyone was eager to meet him. About eight Englishmen from the Admiral stepped over and boarded the Roebuck.

Hidden in the woods, Tamoneok watched as Manteo disappeared onto the ship. Tamoneok sweated with fear for Manteo. He could hear loud laughter and several voices at once. His eyes never left the ships but Manteo and all the strangers were inside the belly of the giant canoe. What in the world is happening out there, he wondered.

Manteo was guided to a chair in front of a crowded table that was full of foods he had never seen. The English gave Manteo a red shirt and showed him how to put it on. Manteo could not wait to show the village his new gift. His eyes searched the faces and objects of the ship. He could understand nothing of the English language and wished he had a gift to give to show his thanks.

"Let's get him drunk!" John proclaimed.

"Yes, give him some wine and meat," suggested another.

Manteo tasted the meat and wine and attempted to show his gratitude through facial expression and hand gestures. The men cheered whenever he drank the wine and, if not for Barlowe, they would have continued to pour it until poor Manteo passed out. Manteo was relieved to find the men friendly and his heart settled. When he was ready to return, he pointed to shore and was returned there by longboat with his red shirt.

Immediately Manteo began fishing out of his canoe with a spear. He desperately wanted to give the visitors something in return for the meal and shirt. The sun was up now and the croaker and flounder were thick near shore. In less than thirty minutes, Manteo had filled his canoe with fish. He divided the fish into two piles and pointed to the two ships and then to the piles of fish. The English had watched Manteo fish, and they were very impressed with his spear fishing ability.

Manteo's visit to the ships and his gifts of fish were the sole topic on board the ships. They wanted to go ashore and find more Indians to trade with. If it was anything like the Caribbean, there were great deals to be made. The ship's officers were cautious and ordered that no weapons should leave their hands in trade or theft. They anticipated more Indians would show up now and felt it was best to stay on the ship and see what the native attitude toward them would be. For now, the men dined on what all agreed was the best fish in the world.

After fishing, Manteo sprinted to the woods to tell Tamoneok what he had seen and show off his red shirt. Manteo was met at the edge of the woods by Tamoneok, who trotted with Manteo back to the village, along with the other villagers who had been watching from the woods.

"What were they like? What did you see?" Tamoneok expected good news and smiled as he ran beside Manteo eager to hear his tale. The red shirt was of the same material as the men from the shipwreck wore years earlier.

"I was deaf to their language as were they to ours but they treated me with all kindness and fed me and gave me gifts. They have lots of wassador (metal). I drank from a wassador cup! There are not that many of them. I counted twenty, and the leader has red hair on his face; it's as red as fire!" Manteo began describing the pork he tasted and the wine. He was very excited. The two men were greeted at the northern edge of the village by Granganimeo. He stood tall and smiled when he saw Manteo pop over a ridge with his red shirt on. He heard the excited young men talking before he saw them and was himself excited and a bit anxious to learn if wassador had been found.

Once again I will insert some quotes from Arthur Barlowe's report that the chapter was based on, complete with the original spelling. Here Barlowe talks about the first ever meeting between the English and Native Americans:

"And after he had spoken of many things not understood by us, we brought him with his owne good liking, aboard the ships, and gave him a shirt, a hat & some other things, and made him taste of our wine, and our meat, which he liked very wel: and after having viewed both barks, he departed, and went to his owne boat againe, which hee had left in a little cove or creeke adjoining: as hee was two bow shoot into the water, he fell to fishing and in less then halfe an houre, he had laden his boate as deepe, as it could swim, with which hee came againe to the point of lande, and there he divided his fish into two parts, pointing one part to the ship, and the other to the pinnesse.."

When Barlowe mentions barks he is talking about the style of ship. A pinnesse is a small ship good for shallow water. A bark has three masts. The foremast and the mainmast are square rigged while the mizzen runs fore and aft.

Copper Crown

Despite an all night rotating watch, no one was spotted on the beach in front of the ships, and no movement was perceived in the thick woods that lined the beach. In the morning, however, the men awoke to see over fifty Indian men sitting on great reed mats on the beach. The Indians sat still and didn't make any noise. Behind them stood about twenty women in a line that ran parallel to shore. Manteo was in his red shirt and called out to the ships in a jubilant Algonquian tongue.

"Look Ben! One of them has on a gold crown." John Wood pointed at Granganimeo who had on a shiny crown that looked like gold. They looked over the crowd of Indians on the beach and found them to be muscular and healthy. Barlowe and Amadas armed themselves with wheel lock pistols and swords and ordered a longboat be loaded with clothes, axes, pewter cups and glass beads to trade. In the West Indies it had been their experience that these items were desired by the natives there. Barlowe, Amadas and four others rowed to shore, while the rest of the English remained on the decks of the ships and watched.

When the English came ashore, Granganimeo and the other men remained seated and smiled. Granganimeo extended his arm, pointing to the land behind him without turning his head, and began to speak to the English who again understood nothing.

'Win-gan-acoa,' which means welcome friend, was mistaken by the English to be the name of the land they were in. Barlowe stood in front of Granganimeo and placed a set of clothes and a tin plate on the reed mat directly in front of

18

him. The plate caused Granganimeo's eyes to open wide and fill with joy. Granganimeo picked it up and clasped it to his chest. In a loud voice, he proclaimed for all to hear that it would protect his heart from his enemy's arrows. Sitting beside Granganimeo was a basket of deerskins, raccoon hides, and pearl necklaces. He nodded to a man sitting on the mat to his right who then picked the basket up and handed it to Barlowe. Barlowe and Amadas sorted through the basket immediately and ordered their men to unload the longboat of their goods.

"This is an even better trade than in the West Indies!" remarked Amadas.

Back on the ship, John and Ben were taking turns shoving each other as they fought for position to look through a recently invented spy glass. It wasn't the items Granganimeo had that interested them, but the twenty or so pairs of uncovered breasts that lined the beach behind Granganimeo.

"My word, look at that one holding the pot on her head! She could gouge an eye out with those pointers."

"Enough Ben! Quit hogging the glass! It's my turn!"

Suddenly, everyone on the beach began to walk southeast along the shore leaving the men left on the ship to wonder what was going on. Granganimeo was leading the English to the old shipwreck, which was half buried in the sand and partially burned.

"No, don't go away topless ladies. What's de urry we just met," John shouted.

Barlowe and the other English were amazed to see the wreckage of an unidentifiable hull. Barlowe pulled out his journal and began to write down the meeting and trade that had just occurred and a description of the shipwreck. As he did this, Manteo spotted the feather in Barlowe's hand

and remembered the image he had seen in the smoke of the fire the night before.

Granganimeo held out two metal rivets that had been taken from the shipwreck and had been tied onto sticks. He then handed them to another man who demonstrated on a nearby piece of driftwood how they were used. The man swung the rivet into the wood like an axe. Amadas nodded his head and walked over to the driftwood. Amadas pulled a hatchet from his waistband and struck it with all his might. The Indians gasped and cheered and immediately began to murmur and talk amongst themselves in a whisper as if that aided in disguising further what they said from the English.

Granganimeo held up his hand and his people fell silent. He then removed a large string of pearls from his neck and held it out to Amadas. Amadas took the necklace and handed Granganimeo the hatchet. All the while, Barlowe recorded everything in his journal. Manteo's eyes never left the feather as he gazed at the black lines made on the paper and wondered their purpose.

"What the devil is going on? Where did they go?" wondered John.

"John, you have asked me that three times now and once again I say, how should I know?" Ben's tone showed his annoyance with his brother.

"Look, they're coming back," said Henry Greene. Henry was a sailor who had gained notoriety as the best shot with a longbow in all of Devonshire. Before taking up sailing, he had been a soldier in the still raging conquest of Ireland.

"My God, look at the amount of goods they are hauling with 'em!" John cried. From the shore, Amadas waved to the ships and shouted for them to come join them. He needed help loading all the new goods. It would take two longboats to tote all of the riches back to the ships. John and Ben boarded another longboat and began rowing to shore. The English now knew what trade items yielded the best return...axes. Everyone wanted to know if the returning party had acquired any gold.

"No gold as of yet. The crown worn by their leader seemed to be copper, for it looked reddish up close. We did however make a small fortune in hides and pearls," Amadas announced to the men as they loaded the longboats.

"Not to mention enough food for a feast." Barlowe unrolled a large buckskin to reveal squash, pumpkins, walnuts, and four deer legs. The squash and pumpkins were new to the English but no one hesitated to take a bite. Another new food item was pagatowr, which later became known as corn. The corn given to the English this day was white, sweet, and short.

The next week was spent trading with the Indians and testing the soil. The English planted peas and beans and watched how the natives planted pagatowr. They toured the village of Croatoan and tried to learn all they could about the new land, despite the language barrier. Manteo, through his constant friendliness and show of endurance, was selected to accompany the English to the mainland and serve as a guide.

Roanoke is an island in the sound northwest of Croatoan. It is 8 miles long and 3 miles wide. Oyster beds surround the island just as they do the sound side of Croatoan. The word Roanoke literally means to make shells smooth. These shells were used locally as a sort of monetary system.

With Manteo's guidance, eight of the English detached from their party at Croatoan to the island of Roanoke and stayed for a few days trading and feasting with the Indians there. It was on Roanoke that it rained for the first time since landing at Croatoan. The English refused to go inside the Indian homes for the night, so the Indians came outside and slept next to the English on reed mats in the rain. The Roanoke Indians traded pearls for glass beads. When held in the sun light, the beads made little rainbows, which fascinated the Indians. To the Roanoke, it seemed like magic.

The English then continued on Northwest to the village of Skico, which is modern day Portsmouth, Virginia. It is here that they heard about Wingina, the paramount chief of the area and Graganimeo's brother. Wingina was wounded in his legs from a recent clash with another tribe, otherwise he would have come to Croatoan immediately upon hearing the news of the English landing and of the wassador they possessed. Everywhere the English went, Manteo followed and each village offered the same trade deals as the Croatoan, and the same warm friendship.

Barlowe and his crew were very pleased with their findings and decided to bring three Natives home with them to introduce to Queen Elizabeth. After approximately seven weeks time, the English headed back to England with their three guests. From the Croatoan, they brought Manteo and Tamoneok and from the Roanoke, they selected a large warrior named Wanchese to travel back to mother England. It was hoped that at least one, if not all three, of the Indians would learn enough English during their winter stay in England, that upon returning to the New World they would be able to negotiate trade deals and be used as interpreters. All three men were excited to see what world was on the other side of the great umpe (ocean).

No gold was found nor silver but the profit from pearls, hides and uppowoc (tobacco) was good enough to warrant another adventure. The Outer Banks provided the perfect geography for privateering. Due to the Gulf Stream running so close to shore off Croatoan, and the naturally shallow sounds and inlets to escape into, the Outer Banks was selected as the perfect spot for the English to build a Navy base to raid Spanish shipping, as well as turn a profit trading with the natives. For the next 300 years, pirates of several nations would infest the same area, including the notorious Blackbeard who would fight to the death at Ocracoke. In addition, German U-boats during both World Wars made the same waters run black with oil and red with blood. Diamond Shoals' insatiable hunger for men and ships only grew stronger once she had her first taste.

Here are a few more excerpts from Barlowe:

"When we shewed him (Granganimeo) all our packet of merchandize, of all things that he sawe, a bright tinne dish most pleased him, which hee presently tooke up and clapt it before his breast, and after made a hole in the brimme thereof and hung it about his necke, making signes that it would defende him against his enemies arrows."

"We exchanged our tinne dish for twentie skinnes, woorth twentie Crownes, or twentie Nobles: and a copper kettle for fiftie skins woorth fifty Crownes. They offered us good exchange for our hatchets, and axes, and for knives, and would have given any thing for swordes: but wee would not depart with any. After two or three dayes the Kings brother came aboord the shippes, and dranke wine, and eat of our meat and of our bread, and liked exceedingly thereof: and after a few dayes overpassed, he brought his wife with him to the ships, his daughter and two or three children: his wife was very well favoured, of meane stature and very bashfull: shee had on her backe a long cloake of leather, with the furre side next to her body, and before her a piece of the same: about her forehead shee had a bande of white Corall, and so had her husband many times: in her eares shee had bracelets of pearles hanging downe to her middle, (whereof wee delivered your worship a little bracelet) and those were of the bignes of good pease. He (Granganimeo) himselfe had upon his head a broad plate of golde, or copper for being unpolished we knew not what metal it should be ..."

"They have no edge-tooles to make them (canoes) withal: if they have any they are very fewe, and those it seemes they had twentie yeres since, which, as those two men declared, was out of a wracke which happened upon their coast of some Christian ship...out of whose sides they drew the nayles and spikes, and with these they made their best instruments. The manner of making their boates is thus: they burne downe some great tree...and putting gumme and rosen upon one side thereof, they set fire into it...they cut out the coale with their shells...very fine boates and such as will transport twentie men."

"He (Granganimeo) was very just of his promise: for many times we delivered him merchandize upon his word, but ever he came within the day and performed his promise. He sent us every day a brase or two of fat Bucks, Conies, Hares, Fish the best of the world. He sent us divers kindes of fruites, Melons, Walnuts, Cucumbers, Gourdes, Pease, and divers rootes, and fruites very excellent good, and of their Countrey corne, which is very white, faire and well tasted, and groweth three times in five moneths: in May they sow, in July they reape, in June they sow, in August they reape: in July they sow, in September they reape: onely they cast the corne into the ground breaking a little of the soft turfe with a wodden mattock, or pickeaxe: our selves prooved the soile, and put some of our Pease in the ground, and in tenne dayes they were of fourteene ynches high: they have also Beanes very faire of divers colours and wonderfull plentie: some growing naturally, and some in their gardens, and so have they both wheat and oates. The soile is the most plentifull, sweete, fruitfull and wholsome of all the worlde: there are above foureteene severall sweete smelling timber trees, and the most part of their underwoods are Bayes and such like: they have those Okes that we have, but farre greater and better."

"...the King himselfe in person was at our being there, sore wounded in a fight which hee had with the King of the next countrey, called Wingina, and was shot in two places through the body, and once cleane through the thigh, but yet he recovered: by reason whereof and for that hee lay at the chiefe towne of the countrey, being sixe dayes journey off, we saw him not at all."

It is possible that the paramount chief was not Wingina but Menatonan, another chief who lived up the Chowan River that the English would meet a year later in 1585 and discover to have lame legs just as the Croatoan said their paramount chief had. When the English finally met Wingina the following year, he was the spitting image of perfect health. To me it seems a strange recovery for a man shot three times, once clean through the thigh to bare no scars. Menatonan, his wife and baby were also found living with the Croatoan in 1587 and the town Menatonan was recovering in was a 6-day journey by canoe from Croatoan. It is however, mentioned in two different primary accounts that Wingina and Granganimeo were brothers. Both, undoubtedly, held some political control probably akin to that of a governor. It is possible that the actual Croatoan chief was Menatonan but that he had recently been defeated by Wingina and had lost some of his territory, and then Wingina placed his brother Granganimeo in charge of the island.

As for the canoes, my Grandmother and her friends found some as children digging forts in the woods on Hatteras. Sadly, they were taken home and used as flower beds or used to sled down the hill and discarded. There were so many canoes and other artifacts that no one knew they were valuable. People filled buckets with arrowheads and sold them for a nickel each to tourists. Other dugout canoes have been found around the state some found near Lake Phelps are over 1,000 years old! It is easy to see how vital canoes must have been to the people of Croatoan. Not only were they used for fishing but also trade and travel. A canoe was the only way to leave the island and the only method for travel other than foot. Remember, that there were no horses in the New World until the Europeans brought them.

The Natives selected to go to England were said to be very healthy and athletic looking. In order to get investors and volunteers for a second voyage, Barlowe needed to demonstrate that the land produced healthy, fit people. In other words, there was plenty to eat in the New World. Scientist and Astronomer, Thomas Harriot, would later suggest the English copy the Croatoan diet because they lived longer and were on the whole taller than the English. Harriot also believed the Indians habit of smoking was "good for the vapors."

Manteo Speaks

-Late summer 1584-

There are no detailed records of the journey back to England in 1584 and that is where Arthur Barlowe's report ends. Barlowe is the only surviving source we have for the 1584 voyage. The next voyage to the Outer Banks from England departs in the Spring of 1585 and lasted almost a year. The two main primary sources for the 1585 voyage come from Sir Richard Grenville and Ralph Lane. You will learn all about both men later in this book and see excerpts from their accounts just as with Barlowe. The next primary source available after Barlowe is the ship log of Tiger, one of seven ships to return to the New World in the Spring of 1585. The following two chapters are mostly narrative and we will pick back up following the primary sources in the chapter Indian Pirates.

Manteo, Wanchese, and Tamoneok bid their families good-bye for an uncertain amount of time. None of them had any idea how long the journey at sea would be. Wanchese and his Indian companions stood with Amadas on the quarterdeck and watched as the islands disappeared. The sun had just risen and made the sky pink and orange. As a result, the water was the same colors only it was mixed with flashes of white from the shoals and bits of grey from hundreds of dolphins that were chasing the ship.

"I hope this rocking stops. I feel as though I just drank some yeopon," Tamoneok said as he attempted to balance himself by putting his hand on the railing. Manteo saw John taking a swig of fire water from a jack cup. He remembered how the men cheered the last time he drank with them and hoped to get the same reaction. Manteo motioned with his hands that he wanted some. John laughed and handed the mug to Manteo who drank three huge gulps.

"Beer. That is beer." John tapped the leather mug with his finger and said the word beer over and over.

"Beeeer," Manteo said slowly imitating John. John began to whoop and shout to all who would listen.

"He spoke! That Indian just said beer! His first English word was beer! Ha ha!"

"Beer," Manteo said as he tapped the mug with his hand. John continued to laugh until Amadas ordered him to man the brace lines on the forecastle, which was near the bow of the ship. John left and could be heard telling everyone that he got Manteo to say beer.

Later that evening, Amadas and Barlowe were sitting with the three guests on the quarterdeck. Barlowe handed Tamoneok some ginger to help with his obvious seasickness. Tamoneok ate a bite and handed it to Wanchese who took a bite, who then handed it to Manteo, who also took a bite. Barlowe held out some tobacco he had acquired trading with the Croatoan and said, "tobacco." Wanchese touched the tobacco with his finger and said, "uppowoc." Barlowe then recorded this in his journal. Next, Barlowe held up some native beads made of shell and bone.

"Minsal, minsal," said Manteo slowly. This process continued for about an hour until each had learned about 30 nouns of the others language.

Manteo seemed to speak the English words the clearest, but he had also been around them the longest. Whenever a word was spoken correctly, Barlowe nodded his head and praised them.

Every day the meals were the same, and the Croatoan were left with nothing to do except during the hour Barlowe spent teaching them English and recording their Algonquian language. To Wanchese, this was hell. Never in his life had he been so idle. One day while observing a man mending a sail on the deck, Wanchese watched what was being done and saw it was not different from sewing he had done before. Wanchese began to help mend the sail and was happy to have something to do. He observed the English getting drunk and watched as their wits left them. He decided not to drink more than he had to in order to stay alive and longed for fresh water. Manteo would drink with the English and even learned to play a flute that was not dissimilar to the ones in Croatoan. Manteo was clearly the favorite of the English.

Tamoneok vomited at least once a day from seasickness and eventually began to sit silent during the English lessons. All three men elected to sleep on the weather deck at night, even if it rained. The stench of the gundeck was too much for them, especially Tamoneok. They were isolated by the language barrier, especially Wanchese. Tamoneok and Manteo were both Croatoan, but Wanchese was Roanoke. He could understand his native companions better than a Spaniard and Portuguese could understand each other, but not much more. Many words were the same but the dialect was different.

They were dressed in English clothes now. They were so far from home that they began to wonder if they would ever see home again. Sadly, one of them would not be returning.

Fishing was one activity that brought some excitement to the crew and the Indians. The favorite bait was flying fish, but most of the time nets were used instead of lines. The water was clear enough that sometimes large schools were easily spotted. The fresh fish were a welcome change to the monotonous diet of ship's biscuits and salted pork. 'Chingwusso' or channel bass were the most fun to catch because on average they weighed fifty pounds, and therefore a single fish could feed the entire crew.

Still, the days and nights seemed to run together and the sea seemed endless to the Indians. Finally, late one evening, land was spotted. The ship's bell rang out and the Indians' hearts raced at the site of land. It was not England, but the uninhabited island of Bermuda. The green mountain peaks and the site of birds filled everyone's hearts with joy, but none more than Tamoneok.

Tamoneok was overtaken by the site of land. He wanted to be off the ship more than anything. He did not wait to board a longboat. As soon as he judged the land near enough to swim to, he jumped overboard and began swimming. The English stood dumbfounded and watched. Tamoneok was a great swimmer but to his surprise, he could hardly stand when he reached the beach. He stumbled as he attempted to run and fell to the sand. The English laughed.

"He's got sea legs, he has!" shouted Henry Greene.

Wanchese was filled with rage. To him, it was not funny. Tamoneok thought he may never walk right again. Moments later, he was fine however and waved to the ships. The men clapped and cheered. Tamoneok sat in the sand and rested after his long swim. Little did he know, the journey had just begun and that Bermuda was only a pit stop for supplies.

Wanchese and Manteo followed Amadas, Barlowe and the ship's pilot Simon Fernando into a longboat. Huge turtles could be seen in the water and on the beach. The water was very warm. A longboat ahead of the one Manteo and Wanchese were in landed first and the men jumped out onto the beach. They immediately captured two large turtles. Turtles are a good source of meat, and they can stay alive for weeks on the ship with very little care. In addition, some of the larger shells could fetch a pretty penny in the black market back in England.

After a short hike from the beach into the tropical forest of Bermuda, the sailors filled casks with fresh water from ponds and dove in for a refreshing swim. Wanchese was happy to have fresh water to drink and enjoyed swimming with the others. Beauty surrounded them. The trees were tall and lush with bright green mosses. The air smelled sweet and a cool breeze swept through the pleasantly warm air.

"So this is where the turtle people come from. I wonder where the rest of them are?" Manteo asked Wanchese. Wanchese said he felt it was not their final destination and said he had seen Amadas with a map that had lines drawn to an island and then the lines continued on to another bigger island farther away. Tamoneok groaned upon hearing this, dreading the thought of being on a ship even longer. Wanchese told him to stop looking at the horizon and lie down on his back and look up at the clouds when on the ship.

The sun would be setting soon and already the men had cut timber and built a fire on the beach. They would be leaving in the morning but not before a night of fun. They had made a small fortune thus far and could not contain their excitement any longer. That night, they danced around the fire while Manteo played the flute. Even Wanchese joined the celebration, but his brief joy turned sour when a clumsy drunk pushed him down. Wanchese sprang to his feet and tackled the man who knocked him down. He then stood and waited for his opponent to rise. It was Ben Wood, who was known to be the best fighter of the company.

The music stopped. The men formed a circle around Wanchese and Ben. Fernando tossed Ben a knife. Ben threw it in the sand and said he didn't need it. Ben fainted a blow at Wanchese then put Wanchese in a headlock. Wanchese lifted Ben off the sand and fell backwards slamming Ben's shoulders to the sand but Ben still held his arm around Wanchese's neck. The sailors shouted things they wanted to see Ben do to Wanchese, especially John.

Wanchese hit Ben with two hooks to the ribs as they both scrambled in the sand. Ben responded by hitting the top of Wanchese's head with his free hand. Wanchese's adrenaline kicked in and he slipped out of the headlock. While still on the ground he lifted a knee into Ben's stomach. Ben let out a groan then rose to his feet. Wanchese too stood up and the men began to cheer even louder. Even Amadas and Barlowe became interested and started to watch.

Wanchese let out a war cry and came in with a jumping knee that was blocked by both of Ben's arms. Wanchese then swung both his fists and hit Ben on both ears simultaneously. Ben was then head butted in the face just as Wanchese landed back on the ground from the flying knee. The men cheered except for John who picked up Fernando's knife. Amadas fired a pistol in the air.

"Drop it John. It was a fair fight." Amadas promised that if there were anymore fights, the combatants would be left in Bermuda after being beaten with a cat of nine tails. Wanchese had just gained a lot of respect from the men. He walked over to Manteo and Tamoneok, covered in sweat, with only a light scratch on his neck. His body was caked with sand but he didn't bother to brush it off. Ben had a bloody lip but decided to drink it off all in good fun. He went back to drinking and singing with his pals. Ben had been in so many scraps that he didn't allow himself to get worked up over it. It was just a scrap, just another scrap.

Wanchese was not mad at Ben but kept his eyes on Fernando. He was angry about the knife Fernando had tossed in. He respected Ben for refusing it. Fernando caught Wanchese staring at him and knew why. He went to Amadas to suggest Wanchese be put in irons for the rest of the voyage.

"That one's dangerous. He cannot be trusted. They're not civilized. We need to teach him respect. You should at least flog him." Fernando spoke in almost a whisper. Amadas shook his head no. Experience had taught him that when someone speaks ill in a whisper, it is subconscious shame. There was no reason to whisper unless attempting to hide a motive.

"He is no harm unless provoked. Besides it will turn the other two against us and all hope of a reliable interpreter will be killed." Fernando did not argue with Amadas. Before becoming a pilot for the English, Fernando had been a Portuguese pirate. He knew his time to strike a blow against Amadas and the others would present itself at a later date. Like a tesicqueo (king snake), Fernando coiled up folding his arms and sat down.

In the morning, the hungover crew rowed back to the ships and set sail again. The rest of the voyage to England was like the voyage to Bermuda, only a bit colder. Manteo, at this time, was the only one making progress with the English language. Tamoneok didn't throw up anymore but still made no attempt to learn English. Wanchese could not understand the English words, but his ever watchful eyes recorded everything he saw. Since he couldn't really speak to anyone, his observation skills were better than they normally were. Wanchese began to lose respect for the English daily. He observed them stealing from each other and cheating at a variety of gambling games.

Finally, England was in site. The ships let off a volley from the pivot guns to announce their return. It was the loudest noise any of the Indians had ever heard. As the ships neared the harbor at Portsmouth, they could see several large ships gathered around. Behind the ships was a maze of docks. There were hundreds of people on the docks and the largest buildings any of the Indians could have imagined. Manteo stood with his mouth agape. He spotted a man onshore riding a horse. He had never seen a horse nor a man riding on the back of any beast.

"Let's stick together and stay out of trouble," Tamoneok said to his native brothers as he looked at all the people on the docks and listened to what seemed like a thousand strange voices. Wanchese stood still, heart pounding and racing as he searched the endless array of new faces. Manteo smiled and held his arm high waving to the strangers. Some of them waved back, but most just stared.

The Hatterasman and the Queen

Barlowe was eager to get to the Queen's court to present his gifts and tell of the New World. It would be a long wagon ride to London with the Indians but a welcome change from rolling around on the ship. Amadas went to Sir Walter Raliegh's home in Devon to bring gifts and discuss the planned military expedition against Spain. The rest of the men got drunk, went home to wives, or visited the red light district.

The horses pulling the wagon amazed the Indians. Manteo pointed to the horses and asked in English, "what this?"

Barlowe smiled and said, "horses." Even Wanchese memorized this word and said it out loud a few times. Tamoneok spotted a wooden sign outside of a tavern that had a picture of a mermaid carved and painted on it. He asked, "Manteo ka ka torawircs yowo?," which means 'how is this called?' in their native tongue.

Barlowe couldn't explain that it wasn't a real creature and therefore only said the word mermaid a few times. The mermaid looked like one of the Indian demigods for both the Roanoke and the Croatoan. A discussion began amongst the three Indians that perhaps the god lived in this part of the world. Barlowe was confused but didn't press the matter.

Barlowe had arranged for some fine English clothes to be sent to the castle to await their arrival. These outfits were for the Indians to wear to the Queens court. The Queen's Court was in London about 60 miles away, which took the men about 4 hours to reach by wagon. The land seemed very hilly and rocky to the Indians.

Upon reaching the palace, the Indians found it strange that the leader lived in a stone lodge that had to be protected by guards. Back home, everyone respected the leaders who lived among the people. Wanchese noticed children outside of these walls wearing rags and begging for food. He did not understand how or why people continued to walk past them and ignore them. Manteo did not see the children because he was busy caring for Tamoneok, who could not stop coughing.

The Indians were led inside by Barlowe past two rows of fancy pants men blowing trumpets. Again, they saw mermaids carved in stone, as well as people with wings on their backs and other creatures they had never seen before. Barlowe handed each of them a set of clothes and led them to a private chamber to change. The floor was covered in a red velvet carpet with gold trim. The Indians' hearts were racing as they put on the clothes. There was a mirror in the room about six feet tall. The only reflection any of them had ever seen was in the surface of water. Manteo slowly approached the mirror and touched it with his finger. All three of the Indians were dressed like gentlemen with ruffled collars and sleeves. Not only were they amazed to see such a perfect reflection of themselves, but also to see themselves in such fancy garb. All three men were silently staring in the mirror when Barlowe came back for them.

"Mirror, Mirror," Barlowe repeated slowly. "Come now it is time to meet the Queen." Barlowe motioned with his hands for the men to follow him. They walked behind Barlowe and into a crowded room full of curiosities.

"Crenepos," whispered Tamoneok to Manteo as he pointed to a group of young ladies dressed to the nines.

"Ah yes. Women, young women. It has been a few months since we have seen them eh?" Barlowe chuckled to himself.

"Wo…men," said Manteo as he winked at a woman wearing a tight corset that made her breasts seem like they might pop out if she sneezed. Barlowe signaled for the men to be quiet.

The Indians followed Barlowe through two large, tall wooden doors with intricate carvings on them. Beyond the doors was an enormous round shaped room with a ceiling twenty feet high. The room was packed with men and women dressed in all sorts of colors and donned with bright hats full of feathers. Most of the men and women were covered from the neck down in garments despite a rather hot day. This seemed very odd to the Indians. Wanchese felt as though his clothes were mildly choking him and walked nervously and slowly behind Barlowe as he looked all around the room. At the far end of the room was a cleared space. Queen Elizabeth sat in the middle of this space on her highly decorated throne. She was dressed in an enormous array of clothes that made her look like an upside down flower to the natives. Her dress had huge white pearls stitched into the several layers of fabric.

The Indians stood for a long time while Barlowe presented a chest of pearls that was brought in by two men who bowed as they opened the chest for the Queen. Many objects that held only moderate value to the Indians were presented one at a time as if they were precious. Manteo spotted a man painting a picture of him and his comrades and held his chest out and stood straight. Suddenly, he heard his name and Barlowe asked him to step forward. Manteo did this and stood still as Queen Elizabeth approached him. She held out a purple cape made of silk. Manteo took the cape and put it on. Next, the Queen gave Wanchese an arrowhead made of silver, and to Tamoneok, a marble pipe with a ship carved on the sides of the bowl.

"Tank you," Manteo smiled as he spoke. The Queen was impressed. The crowd began to clamor.

"Your welcome my dear. Good work, Barlowe. I see you have taught them well."

"Your Majesty, Manteo has by far the best skill for English. He will be a great asset on the return voyage."

"I will part with one ship, the *Tiger,* a fourth rate to accompany whatever fleet Raleigh can put together. What I have seen is good, but do not forget our primary objective. Spain is now a greater threat than ever. We must strike at her source of wealth and strike hard. Hawkins has proved that piracy is a very effective way to do this. As we speak, Sir Francis Drake is doing just that. As soon as the tempest season is over, we will return to the New World and steal the wealth of Spain as we gain wealth and resources ourselves."

The Indians had no idea what was being said and just stood and smiled. "Now, we shall see if the reports from Spain are true. Are the Indians the finest archers in the world? To the range!" The crowd cheered. The three Indians were led outside where the royal archers were practicing shooting targets. The crowd followed behind the Queen.

Outside, Tamoneok was handed a longbow and an arrow by a man with a green hat on. The man pointed to a target of different colored rings about forty yards away. Tamoneok looked at Wanchese and Manteo and said, "Aumoughhowgh?" (A target?) Wanchese nodded yes. Tamoneok understood and fired a shot that hit the bottom of the target. He was not used to such a large bow. Next, an Englishman stepped up and hit the bulls-eye and the crowd erupted into cheers.

Wanchese sighed and took the bow from Tamoneok who continued to cough. The crowed cheered at this gesture and silently waited in anticipation. Wanchese aimed and hit the target about an inch to the right of the bulls-eye. The crowed clapped. Next was another Englishman who sunk an arrow just to the right of Wanchese's. Now it was Manteo's turn. Manteo stepped up and hit the bottom of the bulls-eye. The crowd erupted. Manteo looked at the woman he had winked at earlier and smiled. The woman fanned herself and hid her smile with her fan.

The contest wore on until each Indian had fired three shots and each of the three royal archers had fired three shots. In the end, the royal archers won with a score of twenty-seven to twenty-five. If not for Tamoneok's first shot, the Indians would have won.

After the contest, the men were introduced to Thomas Harriot. He was a scientist and mathematician that they would be living with until it was time to set sail again in the spring of 1585. Harriot was delighted to meet the Indians. Harriot said each of their names as he pointed to them and then said his own name as he pointed to himself. Tamoneok rolled his eyes and continued to cough. Wanchese stood stone-faced and Manteo smiled.

The Indians went on another carriage ride, this time with Harriot and Barlowe. The carriage stopped at Harriot's house just outside of London and he got out followed by his new friends. Wanchese petted one of the horses and was joined by Manteo and Tamoneok. Barlowe remained in the carriage and said good-bye to the men. None of the Indians moved. They were talking among themselves about the horses. Harriot got their attention when his dog came running out to greet them. The men turned their attention to the great dane and the carriage sped off. Harriot petted his slobbery, stupid dog.

"This old boy's name is Basnight. He's friendly, but dumb as a rock." Harriot led his visitors from the New World inside where his cook had prepared a roast beef for them. All the walls of Harriot's house where covered with paintings. The smell of the beef filled their noses and the Croatoan sat down at the table. It seemed as though it would be a very pleasant stay.

Time passed slowly for Wanchese who missed his homeland and native way of life. Manteo, on the other hand, was enjoying his stay and was learning much English from Harriot. However, about a month into their stay, Tamoneok's 'cough' got worse. Initially, Harriot and the doctors thought he had probably contracted whooping cough, but time began to show the truth. He had been coughing daily for weeks, but now he became confined to bed and began to cough up blood, lots of blood. They decided he had contracted tuberculosis while onboard the ship, and his nights spent on the weather deck in the rain had only made matters worse.

Manteo and Wanchese began staying up with him at night and watching him cough continuously. Feeling helpless, they wept and prayed. They longed for their shaman from home, who they felt could cure anything.

One morning, after a long night of coughing and many bloody handkerchiefs later, with an exhausted Wanchese and Manteo by his side, Tamoneok coughed and took his last breath. Wanchese and Manteo fell silent for the rest of the day. They cleaned and prepared Tamoneok's body in the fashion of their tribes and dressed him, while Harriot arranged for a burial and a headstone.

The next day, Tamoneok was buried in England with a grave labeled 'Raleigh' as if his real name was not good enough. The ceremonies seemed strange to Manteo and Wanchese. Back home, they did not put dead bodies in a wooden box. They returned their dead to the Earth in a circular pit to symbolize the circle of life. Tamoneok was the first Native American to die in England. Wanchese was torn in his heart over this strange burial of his friend. He felt it was not right to be buried in this way.

For Wanchese and Manteo, it became a long winter of near isolation with Harriot. Harriot was kind to them and taught Manteo a great deal more English but he was under orders to keep the men safe. Every now and then Harriot would parade his guests in efforts to get investors for another trip to the New World. Manteo and Wanchese had to stand the test of crowded rooms of men in strange clothes all talking at once. Sometimes Manteo would be asked questions and answered in English to the amusement of the room. Wanchese showed that he too had learned some English. Each gathering was the same…a big table was filled with items from Croatoan. The easy exchange of deerskins excited many leather merchants who were eager to get as many as possible for the trade of simple tools. Both Wanchese and Manteo longed for home and the comfort of Crenepos.

One night, Manteo, Wanchese and Harriot had a long talk. Harriot asked if there was meaning behind Manteo's name. Manteo explained that it meant the motion a blue jay makes when it hits its prey. Harriot wrote down 'to snatch'. Wanchese described a bird taking flight off of the water to explain the meaning of his name. Manteo attempted to explain that all of the males in Croatoan were born with one name and then given a new name after a time of trial. The new name was to represent their spirit or soul. The time of trial was a period of isolation in the wilderness with no provisions, usually this occurred around 15 years of age. While in the wilderness, the Great Spirit would reveal to the boy his new name through an epiphany. The young men were supposed to pay attention to the Great Spirit's creations by observing nature and waiting for their new name to be revealed to them. Since a soul never dies, it cannot be represented or contained by a noun it had to be an action. Therefore, almost all of the men on Croatoan had action verbs for their names.

We do know that the Indians were presented at Queen Elizabeth's court and given gifts. We also know that they stayed with Thomas Harriot, that Tamoneok died, and that he really does have a grave in London marked 'Raleigh.' His real name is spelled many different ways but always starts with the letter 'T'. Tamoneok means to sever or to break. It is the closest verb to any of the various spelling of this man's name. Since most men in the tribe had action verbs for names, I chose to use it as his name. Almost nothing is known about the details of the Indians' stay in England. The part about the archer contest comes from William Cummings visit to London with some Cherokee

Indians in the 1700's. I imagine the Croatoan were impressed by the horses and mirrors much the same way as the Cherokees were 120 years later.

Indian Pirates

~Spring 1585~

This chapter is based on the ship journal of the Tiger, the flagship of a fleet of seven English ships that came to the New World in 1585. Excerpts are at the end of the chapter.

It was spring again. Wanchese and Manteo were back in Portsmouth with Thomas Harriot. They understood they were going home and saw some familiar faces onboard the Tiger. Amadas was there, as well as Simon Fernando. The Tiger was four times as big as the Roebuck, had a crew of nearly 300, and sported 28 cannons. This voyage was not the recon mission of 1584. A fleet of seven ships and over 600 men were on their way to the New World. On the way, they would be making a run through the Spanish- occupied Caribbean to pick fights and rob Spanish merchant ships and salt works. This was war.

"**M**armaduke, will you hurry up! You have said your goodbyes to your wife already. Now get on board," the boatswain, John Harris, cried out to a sailor kissing a woman on the dock.

"That wasn't me wife, John. I said goodbye to her back in Devon. That was me mistress," Marmaduke replied as he trotted onboard. He turned and blew a kiss to his mistress, and John shook his head and rolled his eyes.

"Go man the capstan you twisted twit, or help load the last of the cargo. Do something useful," John said in a half joking tone. Manteo and Wanchese were thrilled to be going home. Manteo wanted to help his people benefit from trade with the English and he now understood the language quite well. Wanchese missed his family and the native way of life. They were both in good spirits. Manteo was wearing the cape the Queen had given him and Wanchese kept his · silver arrowhead next to his body in a leather pouch around his neck.

The salt air was whipped up by a stiff breeze, a perfect day for sailing. The boatswain played a lute while the last of the cargo was loaded and was joined by the helmsman, John Cage, on a Spanish guitar. The quartermaster, James Fever, stomped to the tune of the music and sang praises to God asking for a safe journey. Everyone loved James; he was full of life and energy and never seemed to be in a bad mood. Even Wanchese began to nod his head to the beat, and Manteo pulled out his flute and joined in.

The beginning of the journey went off smoothly. The ships stayed in sight of one another with the *Tiger* in the lead. Nothing of great note happened until about a week into the voyage. Somewhere off the coast of Portugal, a storm rolled in. The sails were furled and the men had to ride the hull. Rain blew in sideways and the pumps were constantly manned. The ships rolled and pitched furiously. It was impossible for the ships to stay together and the fleet was scattered.

"We'll make it through. I've seen worse," Fernando said calmly to John Cage who was struggling to man the whip staff and zigzag the ship through the waves. Wanchese and Manteo sat in opposite corners of Harriot's stateroom and braced themselves against the walls with their arms. Harriot was on top of a large cedar trunk full of science equipment, maps, and his writing. At times, he slid around the room on top of the trunk but never fell off or let the trunk slam into the walls. After a few hours, the storm passed and a calm sky with the most amazing rainbow opened up. None of the other ships were visible in any direction, so the *Tiger* fired a cannon to see if it would be answered. About three minutes later, the men heard a distant cannon shot, but by which ship no one knew for sure. The *Tiger* pressed on alone believing that the ships would rendezvous at Puerto Rico as planned. The rest of the way to Puerto Rico went well. In fact, it went better than well.

"Spanish ship off the starboard. Looks to be a small merchant vessel!" shouted Darby Gland, an Irishman pressed into service against his will. He was out on the ship's head relieving himself when he spotted the ship.

All at once, the men fanned out to the gun-ports and began to crack them open. The ports had been sealed shut with tar and hemp to keep seawater out. Richard Grenville was the man in charge (he was also a cousin of Sir Walter Raleigh). Grenville ordered Ralph Lane, a professional soldier and ruthless brute, to fire a warning shot once they got in range. Catching up to the Spanish ship was easy for the *Tiger* was much faster. A single shot was fired and the honor was given to Darby for spotting the ship. The shot sailed over the bow of the Spanish ship and they immediately struck up a white flag.

"Dat's for interruptin' me privy time, ya no-good vagabonds!" Darby shook his fist as he spoke and the men in his gun crew laughed. The prize was carrying a cargo of cloth mostly, which in the New World could be traded for far more valuable goods. They loaded the cargo onto the *Tiger*, and then Grenville ordered the ship be manned by a prize crew and turned back to England. The *Tiger* had more than enough men on board for just such a purpose. Manteo recognized the Spanish flag from the old wreck in Croatoan. A flag just like it sat inside the common hut in his village folded into a triangle on a reed mat. *So they are enemies,* he thought to himself.

Not an hour later, another ship was spotted, but this one gave chase and would not surrender so easily. After the

English fired a warning shot, she fired back with two small cannons that managed to come close to scoring hits. Columns of water rose out of the sea forty feet into the air from the near misses and wet the deck.

"Load grape shot and rip her sails and rigging. We don't want to sink her if we can capture her." Ralph Lane wasn't threatened by the tiny ship. Even if the shots had hit the *Tiger* they would not have penetrated her thick oak hull. The men did as ordered and managed to rip up the sails and some of the rigging. No one was killed or wounded on either side, and again a white flag was raised by the Spanish. The Spanish crew was placed in irons and her officers in double irons. The cargo this time was next to nothing because she had just unloaded her cargo of molasses and was on her way to another island to pick up salt. The ship itself however was a pretty penny and again was manned by a prize crew and sent to England. The Spanish officers and crew were kept on the *Tiger* to be used as a ransom for pigs and goats once Puerto Rico was reached. The English planned to steal horses there and wait for any other ships of their own fleet that may arrive.

At last, their destination was in sight. Manteo and Wanchese were playing dice with Marmaduke and another man named Rodger Dean. Rodger was a big fellow. His arms had been made strong from blacksmithing. Marmaduke, like most sailors, was wiry and tough but had the face of a teenager. At heart he was not a sailor but a fisherman and a good one. All four men were on the gundeck when John Harris began to shout, "Land ho!"

The ship anchored close to shore and the men took the longboats stuffed with provisions to shore. They were planning on staying for about two weeks, so the men built a fort next to a pond that was full of large crabs. John White, an artist sent to paint pictures of the New World, painted an aerial view of this fort. During their stay, soldiers were sent across the island to rob and trade with the Spanish settlers.

They were mainly after livestock and managed to acquire many horses and cattle. Manteo and Marmaduke spent the dawn sky catching and shelling the crabs from the pond adjacent to the fort. The rest of the day, Marmaduke had other duties such as digging to create earthworks and helping to refill casks with fresh water. Fresh fruit was abundant and everyone ate plenty to prevent getting scurvy. Manteo and Wanchese helped wherever they could, preferring to work and use their muscles, rather than be sedentary.

No one knew the fate of the other six ships, but all began to wonder out loud after the first week.

"I wonder what happened to the rest of the ships?" commented Grenville.

"I imagine they may have pushed forward on to Croatoan," replied Harriot.

It wasn't all fun and games at Puerto Rico. Grenville ordered that another ship be built in haste to replace any that may have been lost in the storm off Portugal. This ship was to be loaded with goods traded for or stolen from the Spanish colonists.

Nine days into their stay, the *Elizabeth,* a ship from their fleet, came sailing in. It was a welcome sight to see one of their ships. That night, the men threw a huge party. The wine and beer flowed and the music played into the wee hours of the night. Occasionally, someone would fire a round into the warm night air. The men were far from home and had already captured two ships, stolen horses from various parts of the island from helpless Spanish colonists, and exchanged their Spanish prisoners for pigs and goats. A few of the pigs were roasting over the beach fires at the party.

Manteo was enjoying this new adventure in Puerto Rico. He was often heard playing his flute and was loving the taste of fresh hot crabs after enduring the harsh, salty meals served on the ship. Wanchese on the other hand was growing impatient. Were they not returning to his homeland as Harriot had said? When would they be departing again?

Despite his frustration, Wanchese did not fight during his stay in Puerto Rico.

Once the new ship was complete, it was time to press on. The Tiger, the Elizabeth, and the new ship loaded up their cargoes and headed west. All of the men wondered about the fate of the other 5 ships.

There was another quick stop to rob a salt works on an uninhabited island near Puerto Rico, a trip that lasted half a day. The salt was badly needed to keep their meats from spoiling and was also worth a lot of money back in England.

The Elizabeth, the Tiger, and the new ship would not stop again until Wokokon, an island just south of Croatoan (modern day Ocracoke). This stop, however, was not planned. Despite the sailors' best efforts to take soundings with a leading line (check the depths with a lead weight tied to a rope), the Tiger would come to a grinding halt, running aground in shallow sand that popped up out of nowhere directly off of Wokokon. It was the Island's way of saying: Welcome to the Outer Banks.

Here are some excerpts from Richard Grenville, captain of the 1585 voyage and cousin to Sir Walter Raleigh. Once again I have left the original spelling and grammar:

The 9. day of April, in the yeere abovesayd, we departed Plymmouth, our Fleete consisting of the number of seven sailes, to wit, the Tyger, of the burden of seven score tunnes, a Flie- boat called the Roe-bucke, of the like burden, the Lyon of a hundred tunnes or thereabouts, the Elizabeth, of fiftie tunnes, and the Dorothie, a small barke: whereunto were also adjoyned for speedy services, two small pinnesses.

The 29. {April}) day wee set saile from Saint Johns, being many of us stung before upon shoare with the Muskitos: but the same night wee tooke a Spanish Frigat, which was forsaken by the Spaniards upon the sight of us, and the next day in the morning very early we tooke another Frigat, with good and rich fraight, and divers Spaniards of account in her, which afterwards wee ransomed for good round summes, and landed them in S. Johns.

The 26. [June} we came to anker in Wocokon.

The 29. {June} wee weighed anker to bring the Tyger into the harbour, where through the unskilfulnesse of the Master whose name was Fernando, the Admirall strooke on ground, and sunke.

Wocokon is the old name for Ocracoke Island and was often spelled Wokokon, which means sacred or one who flys around. A shipwreck is a fitting start for the arrival of the fleet. The Outer Banks are home to over 8,000 shipwrecks today.

Welcome to Wokokon

~Late July 1585~

Unbeknownst to the Tiger, the Elizabeth, and the new ship, four of the other ships from their fleet, including the Roebuck and the Dorothy, were already anchored off of Croatoan, and had been there for 20 days already, waiting for the Tiger to show up. Thirty-two men from these ships had already gone ashore and begun construction of a series of forts along the beach guarding the inlets north of Croatoan. Unbeknownst to all of the men was the fact that the one missing ship was lost off Portugal due to the ship's captain running the ship ashore on purpose and disposing most of the crew there so he could go pirating on his own accord. The storm allowed him a chance to do this without the other ships knowing until he was long gone. However, with the new ship built in Puerto Rico, seven total ships did arrive in the New World, even though it was not the original seven and not all on the same day. The men from these ships spent their time at Croatoan trading goods, shooting birds and catching fish. The Croatoan shared their food and treated the English like brothers.

Wokokon was a beautiful sight to the returning Natives. Manteo and Wanchese were both anxious to be home and see their families. Manteo could see his island on the horizon to the North and knew it would not be much longer before he was home. Wanchese thought about pulling a Tamoneok but knew he would drown. The waters here were as deadly as any in the world. The land seemed quiet and still in comparison to the cities they had been in for the past nine months. The beauty of the pelicans gliding through the air and the dolphins gliding through the water was surreal. Home never looked so good, so peaceful.

The three ships were gliding along smoothly, moving north towards Croatoan, when Marmaduke hollered out from the top of the ships forecastle, "Ahoy! Two ships dead ahead!" Everyone immediately clamored to the front of the ship, only to see two, then three, then four of the vessels from their fleet off the coast of Croatoan. The men began to whoop and cheer with excitement.

Suddenly, the ship came to a grinding halt, and all the men lurched forward. The *Tiger,* being the largest of the fleet, had the deepest draft and therefore ran aground while the *Elizabeth* and the new ship did not.

The *Tiger* was a scene of chaos. Upon running aground, some charcoal was flung out of the cook box onto the deck and had caught a mop on fire. The fire quickly started to spread to a nearby coil of rope. James Fever bravely picked up the flaming mop and tossed it overboard. He then stomped out the fire with help from several others around him. This little episode was the least of their problems though. Water was leaking into the cargo hold and spoiling much of the stolen salt. The men needed this salt to cure meat and therefore a lot of the food was lost.

While the men scrambled around the ship salvaging what they could and trying to lighten the ship, it was decided to throw some of the heavy cargo overboard, including some of the ballast rocks and one sick cow. They also decided to lighten the load by sending a few men to Croatoan to get word from the Englishmen who had been waiting there for the *Tiger* to arrive.

Manteo and Wanchese were sent to the south end of Croatoan in a longboat to begin trade negotiations and renew the old friendship that had existed in 1584. Accompanying them was the scholar Harriot, an artist named John White, Marmaduke and Rodger.

"I don't know about you, Rodger, but I am happy to be selected to be rowing this boat ashore. Tempers onboard were starting to flare," Marmaduke said as he kept up a steady row. Rodger agreed and both were anxious to see first hand about all the topless women they had heard tale of. John White and Harriot were having their own conversation in the bow of the ship and Manteo and Wanchese grabbed a pair of oars and helped row. No one wanted to get to the island worse than Wanchese. He wanted to shed his English clothes and return to his old way of life as soon as he hit the shore. He viewed the English as a threat. Manteo saw the English as a means to learn new skills and benefit his people with trade and technology. Both men were right.

"Manteo, when we reach the shore, I am heading straight home to my family. Do not trust these men. They will take everything if they can. They brought many weapons with them this time," Wanchese spoke in his native tongue.

"On your way home, stop in my village and tell them we have returned. Someone there will take you home by canoe. I plan to trade with and learn from these men. Perhaps they will help us defeat our enemies. They will rely on us for food for they are not a people of the land. They cannot be our enemies because they will come to need us," replied Manteo. All the while, the English were deaf to their conversation.

The longboat reached the beach and Wanchese took off his shirt and breeches and sprinted into the woods. Harriot called out to him and Manteo put his hand on Harriot's shoulder. Manteo shook his head no and said, "Wanchese go home, family." Harriot understood but sighed. After dragging the longboat further onto the shore, the men followed Manteo into the woods. Marmaduke picked up the shirt Wanchese had discarded and held it to his body.

"Sorry Rodger, but this will fit me perfectly."

"You should trade it once we reach the village. You can buy ten of them back home with the goods you will get," Harriot spoke with confidence. Marmaduke and Rodger looked at each other and grinned. John White had his paints and canvas with him and was eager to start his water colors. He had already done paintings of the fort at Puerto Rico and of the Spanish salt works they robbed on the way over. He painted every new fish, bird, and plant they came across and Harriot recorded their native names and wrote descriptions of their use and quantity. Manteo told Harriot the names and answered his questions as best as he could.

While walking to the Croatoan village on the northwest end of Buxton on Hatteras Island, the men came across a funny-looking animal with a ringed tail about the size of a beaver. Harriot asked what it was and Manteo thought he asked what the animal was doing. "Raccoon," which means 'to scratch' was therefore mistakenly recorded as the name of the animal. Next they saw an animal hanging upside down. The same mistake was made so "opossum," which means 'to carry in a pouch' was recorded as that animal's name.

The Croatoan had already spotted the other four ships off shore and word had already been sent to tell chief Wingina. In addition to much exchange of goods with the English, a huge feast and celebration were being planned by the Natives in a principal village called Secotan. (Secotan is where present day Belhaven, NC is located and means 'burnt ground').

Wanchese reached Manteo's village in record time and told them of Manteo's return. He was escorted home in a canoe as Manteo had said he would be. Upon hearing the news from Wanchese, Manteo's mother and four others decided to head south and meet Manteo along the path leading to the village. They brought a plucked and cooked trumpet goose and a basket of apples covered in black cinnamon, which was Manteo's favorite treat.

Manteo met his family along the path. He was ecstatic to see his mother. He ran up and hugged his mother
lifting her off the ground. His people were surprised to see
his purple cape. Of all the dyes, purple was the most revered
for it came from the animal inside of the whelk shell. The
whelk shell was used as a tool for making canoes and a
symbolic cup used to drink yaupon tea during ceremonies.
The Indians all gathered around Manteo, touching his cape
and admiring his English clothes. Manteo's mother told
about the Englishmen from the other ships arrival weeks ago
and how they wondered if he was ever coming back. Manteo
then explained about Tamoneok. For once, it was the English
and not Manteo who stood listening to a strange language
wondering what was being said.

Meanwhile, an armada of longboats from the *Elizabeth* and the *Tiger* were making their way through the inlet
between Wokokon and Croatoan Island. The other 4 ships
remained anchored off Croatoan and Hatorask to the north.
They were unaware of the *Tiger*'s plight but began to
wonder if something was wrong. Spearheading the little fleet
of longboats was Ralph Lane and Philip Amadas. Amadas
remembered from his voyage the year before hearing a tale
of a lake full of pearls named Paquiyup. Since they had come
in directly across the sound from where this lake was
supposed to be, he wanted to search it out. He had spent a
year dreaming about the riches there. Before heading to this
'pearl lake,' however, he wanted to ask Manteo to come
along to help interpret for him.

Amadas, Lane, and the other longboats landed at
Croatoan and sounded a trumpet to call for Harriot.
Marmaduke, being the most fleet of foot, was sent back to
the beach to see what Amadas wanted. The rest of the group
sat feasting on the goose and apples while waiting in the
woods for Marmaduke's return. John White was painting a
portrait of Manteo's mother while Rodger and Harriot were

filling themselves with the cinnamon apples freely given to them when Marmaduke came running back from the beach.

"Master John Arundel says we have to go with them to the mainland right away and he wants Manteo to come and interpret. Orders are from Grenville himself. Master Harriot please tell Manteo that he will be brought back here after a week on the mainland but that he must come. Amadas is hell-bent on reaching some magic lake he heard tale of the last time he was here."

Harriot and John White were disappointed to be leaving so soon and felt bad for Manteo. John folded up the painting he had just begun with a huff. Harriot didn't know how to tell Manteo what was going on and hesitated to say anything. Manteo surprisingly had understood everything Marmaduke had said and was already explaining it to his people. He was willing to go, but his family was heartbroken. He gave them his cape and headed back to the beach with the Englishmen.

Pearl Lake

The voyage across the sound was a quick one because the wind was at their backs. The little sprit sails of the longboats pulled them across in a straight line. The mainland was flat and full of pine trees, cedars, and similar wildlife to that of Croatoan. The first village the English came to sat on the sound and was called Pomieok, which means 'place to land boats easily'. Here, John White finally had time to paint. He painted the entire village complete with the palisade that went around it and a group of natives dancing around a fire in the center of the village. The village looked like Croatoan with many longhouses covered in reeds and bark. Fields of crops grew all around the village.

The English were greeted by a man and a woman. The man and the woman spoke with Manteo, who explained they had come to trade with them and see the lake. The people of Pomieok told Manteo that word had already reached them about the turtle people's return. They told him about the feast at Secotan that was being prepared and how the chief, Wingina, was in Aquscogoc. (Aquscogoc means to disembark.). Manteo said he would take the white men to Aquscogoc after they had seen the lake.

The woman sent two young warriors to guide Manteo and the English to the lake and returned to Pomieok herself. Luckily, Aquscogoc was only about ten miles away. There would be two feasts now, one at Aquscogoc and one at Secotan.

The English were led to the lake that remained un-
seen until at the waters edge. The forest around the lake was
very thick. Amadas reached the shore of the lake and stood
transfixed. The water was a turquoise color and the light
sparkled off the surface. The lake did not contain any more
oysters than in the sound, far less in fact, but it did contain
the largest blue crabs any of the English had ever seen. The
two warriors from Pomieok demonstrated how easily the
crabs were caught by spearing a few for the English.
Marmaduke licked his lips and stared wide-eyed at the crabs.
They were huge! Amadas asked Manteo about pearls.
Manteo told him there were no large oyster beds in the lake
but Amadas was not satisfied.

After making his men search the lake for oyster beds
for an hour and finding none, Amadas grew impatient.
Manteo saw this and told Harriot they could trade for pearls
at the next village and that a feast was being prepared for
them there. Harriot relayed the news. Hearing this, Lane told
Amadas that they would be leaving for the next village
immediately.

Aquscogoc was crowded with villagers from Pomieok and Secotan waiting with baskets of goods to trade
with the English. The English were showered with gifts of
deerskins and other hides. Turkeys were roasting and squash
and pumpkins lined a long reed mat. Everyone ate until they
could hardly stand and as promised, the Natives had many
pearl necklaces to trade. In exchange, the English handed out
tin plates, wooden beads, and hatchets. They even brought
dolls for the children and played music together with the
Indians. Manteo did a fine job interpreting and, as always,
Harriot recorded everything he could. John White painted
pictures of the shamans, or medicine men, and a few of the
native women with their young children. The women and
men both only wore skins and some had white and green
circles painted on their legs and arms. Most wore shell
jewelry or pearls. A few had copper ornaments and feathers.

Manteo was surprised that Wingina was not around, and heard that Wingina was on his way to Roanoke Island to order his people there to give the town and the island to the English. This way the English would be somewhat separated from any of his villages. He had given permission to his people to trade with the English and asked that all friendliness and generosity be shown to their new friends.

All the while, Grenville and the other Englishmen were still working to get the Tiger off the sandbar. Contact had been made with the rest of the fleet anchored off of Croatoan, and orders had been given that they were to continue to work on the series of forts that stretched from a place called Kindrick's Mount (Salvo) north to the mouth of an inlet they named Port Fernando. A small look-out fort was hastily constructed on the north end of Roanoke Island as well, but the fort at Port Fernando was to be the best armed and the biggest. The English were taking no chances with the Spanish. They would not end up like the French slaughtered at Fort Caroline twenty years before down in Charleston SC. For the time being, the English were fanned out across the Outer Banks and inland river towns.

This chapter is based on the Tiger's Journal, headed by Richard Grenville and John White's actual paintings. Also included are facts taken from Thomas Harriot's 'Brief and True Report,' published in 1590. The English really did visit all the towns mentioned and were treated with kindness by all of the Native Americans they met. Here are more excerpts from the Tiger Journal:

The 6. M. John Arundel was sent to the maine, and Manteo with him: and Captaine Aubry and Captaine Boniten the same day were sent to Croatoan, where they found two of our men left there with 30. other by Captaine Reymond, some 20. dayes before.

The 8 Captaine Aubry and Captaine Boniten returned, with two of our men found by them, to us at Wocokon.

The 11. day the Generall accompanied in his Tilt boate with Master John Arundell, Master Stukeley, and divers other Gentlemen, Master Lane, Master Candish, Master Hariot, and twentie others in the new pinnesse, Captaine Amadas, Captaine Clarke, with ten others in a shipboat, Francis Brooke, and John White in another shipboate, passed over the water from Wococon to the maine land victualled for eight dayes, in which voyage we first discovered the townes of Pomejok, Aquascogoc and Secotan, and also the great lake called by the Savages Paquipe, with divers other places, and so returned with that discovery to our Fleete.

The 12. we came to the Towne of Pomeiok.

The 13. we passed by water to Aquascogok.

Silver Cup

Only one night was spent in Aquascogoc. The next day, the English traveled southwest to Secotan where an even bigger party awaited them.

The sail from Aquscogoc to Secotan was easy, for the wind was still favorable and the river was calm. It took most the day to reach Secotan, but as promised, Secotan provided an even greater feast than Aquscogoc. In addition, even more goods were exchanged between the English and the Natives. John White painted a picture of this village as well with its surrounding fields of various crops. The mood was friendly. Again, there was much dancing and celebration.

At some point during the festivities, Ralph Lane discovered he was missing a silver cup. He was outraged and claimed that someone had stolen it. He figured it must have been stolen during the night they spent in Aquscogoc. While the men were dancing to the Indian drums and English lutes, Lane called Amadas to meet with him privately.

"These savages have stolen a silver cup from us. This will not be tolerated. Take fifteen men and return to Aquscogoc and raise it. Burn the village and the fields that surround it." Lane spoke with a vicious tone. Even battle-hardened Amadas thought this order was a bit much. The people of Aquscogoc had given away enough food and gifts to pay for the cup a hundred times over, and many of them had traveled to Secotan to participate in yet another celebration with the English. Amadas obeyed orders without any resistance, keeping his opinions to himself.

Amadas and the fifteen men hurried back to the village of Aquscogoc and did as they were told and spared nothing. The reed houses burned quickly filling the air with smoke and illuminating the night sky. The few villagers who were still there fled in fear. They were confused as to why the English would do such a thing after they had celebrated their arrival. The burning of their grain fields angered them more than the loss of their dwellings because crops were harder to replace and more valuable.

It was dark now and Manteo was playing a flute in Secotan, dancing around a fire while Aquscogoc was burning. He, along with most of the English, had no idea what was going on.

About midnight, as the party was starting to wind down, Marmaduke spotted Amadas returning from the edge of the woods bordering the village of Secotan. Amadas had on his armor and was looking somber. Marmaduke sat eating a turkey leg, as he watched Amadas walk straight up to Lane. He could not hear what was said, but he saw Lane smiling and laughing.

Suddenly, the English were ordered back to the longboats by Lane. The men stood around confused, which angered Lane.

With a strip of succulent turkey meat hanging out of his mouth, Marmaduke leaned over to Rodger and said, "Is he serious? I think he needs his ticker checked."

Rodger just slowly shook his head side to side, woozy from all the wine and food.

Lane shouted his orders again and the men left in haste accompanied by Manteo. Harriot had heard about the burning of Aquscogoc and was disgusted. He waited until they had reached the longboats before he told Manteo. Manteo's reaction was hard for Harriot to read. He sat very still, looking completely emotionless.

Once the men were in the longboats and well on their way back to the ships, Lane told them what had happened.

"We are returning to the ships and heading north to help construct the forts. A silver cup was stolen by the savages at the village of Aquscogoc, and thus it has been burned to ashes." Lane stood in front of the longboats as he spoke and got a reaction of silence. Many of the men looked down at their feet in shame, as their bellies still felt full of the foods from the feasts, and their pockets were full of treasures. Lane then lifted the lid of an entire chest of pearls to look at his treasures that he had gotten for trading a copper kettle. In his mind, he was comforted by the fact that the Indians were not Christians. To him this meant they were less human, soulless and certainly not equals.

The men sailed back across the sound under a full moon. The air was warm and the breeze was light. It would be near dawn before the men returned to Wokokon where the *Tiger* still sat grounded on the sandbar.

Once they reached the ships Lane boarded the Tiger to meet with Grenville. Grenville informed Lane that he would be departing with all of the ships and all but 105 of the men. Lane would be left in charge and Grenville promised to return within three or four months laden with supplies. Lane was happy to be free of Grenville whom he hated. Grenville left Lane two pinnaces or small ships about 40 feet in length and 20 longboats.

Lane immediately ordered his men onto the pinnaces and to dissemble the longboats to take with them on the pinnaces. They were heading north. They made it as far as Hatorask before stopping to rest. Hatorask was the island just north of Croatoan, where modern day Pea Island is. By the time they reached Hatorask, the men were exhausted. The men were sent ashore to rest.

On the beach at Hatorask, most of the men were still a bit drunk from the party at Secotan and slept in the sand despite the mosquitoes. Marmaduke and Rodger swatted ever present mosquitoes and talked about the goods they had obtained in trade. The sun was peeking over the ocean now and the moonlight symphony of frogs, crickets and owls was beginning to fade. The men awoke to a horn blown by Lane after about only four hours of rest.

"To the boats lads! It is time to get to work." Lane was in his armor and stood tall yelling at the men to hurry. "We are heading to Port Fernando to work on the main fort. Professional soldiers of the fleet have already transferred some heavy cannon to that location and have already begun the process of building the fort." (Port Fernando was near the modernday Bodie Island Lighthouse).

Upon arrival at the fort, any men who were not sol-diers were ordered to stay in the longboats and proceed to the Island of Roanoke, which could be seen a short distance away in the sound. This included Marmaduke and Rodger, who were relieved to be free of Lane's relentless dictatorship for a while. Their Captain, Edward Stafford was a much more reasonable man.

Manteo was sent with Amadas and 20 others to Dasamonquepeu, a village on the mainland west of Roanoke Island aboard one of the pinnaces. Wingina was said to be there, and word had it that Wingina was angry about the burning of the village. Lane wanted Manteo to go and interpret for Amadas to gather information from Wingina and inform him he was to pay tribute to Lane his new master. Lane stayed at Port Fernando and surveyed construction for a short while, but eventually loaded himself and forty men into the other pinnace to follow Amadas over to Dasamonquepeu.

Dasamonquepeu means peninsula in Algonquian and was in the area between modern day Mashoes and Mann's harbor.

The Tiger was afloat again and headed back to the West Indies to rob more Spanish ships. Grenville left with the Tiger, which left Ralph Lane in command. Lane was out to make a name for himself. He resented that Grenville had been selected as the leader of the expedition, and he secretly sent two of his henchmen back to England on the Tiger with letters complaining about Grenville. Lane was planning to force the Indian nations to serve the English and was planning to use a despicable tactic to do so. His plan was to learn who the leaders of the tribes were, kidnap them and hold them for ransom until he was given the location of the pearl beds. In addition, he planned to force the tribes to pay him a daily tribute in food and other gifts. Lane had previously shown his ruthlessness in Ireland where he had killed off entire villages and tortured some of his victims.

More excerpts from the Tiger's Journal that the last 3 chapters were based on:

The 15. we came to Secotan, and were well enter-tained there of the Savages.

The 16. wee returned thence, and one of our boates with the Admirall was sent to Aquascogok, to demaund a silver cup which one of the Savages had stollen from us, and not receiving it according to his promise, wee burnt, and spoyled their corne, and Towne, all the people being fled.

The 18. we returned from the discovery of Secotan, and the same day came aboord our Fleete ryding at Wococon.

The 21. our Fleete ankering at Wococon, we wayed anker for Hatoraske.

The 27. our Fleete ankered at Hatorask, and there we rested.

The 29. Grangino brother to king Wingina came aboord the Admirall, and Manteo with him.

The 2. the Admirall was sent to Weapomeiok.

The 5. M. John Arundell was sent for England.

The 25. our Generall wayed anker, and set saile for England.

The burning down of Aquascogoc and the adjoining fields is certainly significant and will play a huge role in events to come later in the story. It is possible that John White, the famous painter and Governor of another colony in 1587, never visited Roanoke Island in 1585. Interestingly, all of John White's paintings of the New World are of towns from the Mainland or of people from those towns. None of John White's paintings are of Roanoke Island and not once in the Tiger Journal is it mentioned that any Englishman ever set foot on Roanoke. We know that 32 Englishmen had been on Croatoan for 20 days before the Tiger arrived. We know the English spent some time at Hatorask (Rodanthe, NC today) and that they visited towns on the North bank of the Pamlico River but those are the only places the Journal mentions the English visited in the first six weeks after arrival.

It is quite possible that John White, who we know was on a ship with Francis Brooke, remained with that ship, meaning he arrived on the 29th of June and departed on the 5th of August before anyone had gone to Roanoke Island. Brooke's ship visited Pomeiok, Aquascogok and Secotan. We have detailed John White watercolors of the villages of Pomeiok and Secotan and paintings of villagers from Aqauscogok. John White is not mentioned again in any of the sources for the 1585 voyage.

The rest of what we know about the English stay in the New World in 1585 comes from Captain Ralph Lane. Lane was in charge after Grenville departed with all of the large ships and 495 of the 600 men. Lane's account is very important to understand and is probably the most detailed primary source to survive. We will take a close look at Lane's writings a few chapters from now. As the next few chapters are based on his account.

Insane Lane

The Pinnace arrived at Dasamonquepeu with Manteo, Amadas, and twenty others. Directly behind them were Lane and his forty men, outfitted in armor as if for battle. They landed on the mainland west of Roanoke Island.

Lane introduced himself to Wingina by using Manteo as an interpreter and demanded tributes of grain and pearls to be paid everyday. He also asked where the next closest ruler could be found so that he could demand his tribute as well. Wingina was shocked and angered but smart enough to size up the situation when he saw all the well armed men Lane had with him. He remembered the cruelty they had already shown. Wingina told Manteo that he would do as Lane asked, but also told Manteo to take Lane to see Menatonan. Menatonan was a powerful chief, and Wingina full of contained rage, planned to rid the world of Lane after all. Wingina paid his first day's tribute with a smile by sending a messenger to the nearest village to fetch the grain and things Lane demanded. He then described through Manteo's interpretation how to get to Chowanoke where Menatonan lived. Lane was pleased and decided he would go to Chowanoke immediately after his shipment of grain and other gifts arrived.

What Lane did not know was that Wingina also told his messenger to send word to warn Menatonan and the neighboring chief of the Mandoags, that Lane was on his way to destroy them. The Mandaog, which means stealthy or snake like, were said to mine copper from a river and had over 700 bows they could bring against the English.

Manteo was left in the dark about Wingina's warning, for Wingina did not know if he could trust Manteo.

Lane was starting to become impatient waiting for his tribute when suddenly some of Wingina's men arrived with several bushels of grain and many hides and pearls.

"Wise choice old man. Let's see if your heathen neighbors are as wise as you." Lane packed up his goods in his pinnace and they set sail up the river with Manteo, Amadas, forty soldiers, and a guide that Wingina had provided since Manteo did not know how to get to Chowanoke. The English took some of the food from Wingina's tribute with them and sent the rest to Roanoke in small boats with the twenty men Amadas had brought with him.

It was over a week to get to Chowanoke often rowing against the current of the river.

Some excerpts from Ralph Lane's report:

"Chawanook it selfe is the greatest Province & Seigniorie lying upon that River, and the very Towne it selfe is able to put 700. fighting men into the fielde, besides the force of the Province it selfe.

The King of the sayd Province is called Menatonon, a man impotent in his lims, but otherwise for a Savage, a very grave and wise man, and of a very singular good discourse in matters concerning the state, not onely of his owne Countrey, and the disposition of his owne men, but also of his neighbours round about him as well farre as neere, and of the commodities that eache Countrey yeeldeth. When I had him prisoner with me, for two dayes that we were together, he gave mee more understanding and light of the Countrey then I had received by all the searches and Savages that before I or any of my companie had had conference with:"

Ralph Lane was obsessed with finding gold, copper or the source of the best pearls. He wanted to know the locations of natural resources and was willing to do anything to get them.

The Mandoag Sing

Where the other 65 men were exactly, while Ralph Lane and 40 of his soldiers were pushing up the river toward Chowanoke is unclear but some were on Roanoke Island.

After days of seeing no one, Lane and his crew's food was beginning to run out and they had to ration themselves. Upon reaching Chowanoke, they saw a large force of men with bows and arrows, clubs, and wooden swords gathered around talking in an open grass field. When the Chowanoke saw the ship, they ran into the woods or behind the houses of Chowanoke. The Mandoags had not yet arrived but the Chowanoke force alone outnumbered Lane's.

Lane ordered the deck gun loaded with grape shot. He had no heavy cannon on board because he had positioned all of them at the various forts he had built from Hatorask to Roanoke.

"Give fire!" Lane shouted. Lane personally aimed the gun as the wick of the gun was lit by another man who touched it with a slow burning match. The sound of the gun caused many of the Indians to be gripped with fear. Manteo and the guide sent by Wingina cringed as they saw nine Indians wounded and two killed. One man had been struck by four different pieces of shot and his blood stained the grass red. The English stormed onto the shore with full armor on and an assortment of small arms. A few arrows struck their armor and bounced off harmlessly. The bark of their guns so frightened the Natives that most of them fled into the woods, but not Menatonan. Among the smoke and noise, Menatonan spotted Manteo standing by the ship, clutching a gun to his chest obviously frightened. Menatonan called out to Manteo to please ask them to stop. He would surrender to their wishes. Manteo shouted this message nervously to Lane two or three times before Lane listened and called off his men.

Lane asked Manteo, "which one is Menatonan?" Manteo pointed to a man that was sitting on a wicker mat covered with a deer hide outside of a reed and birch bark house.

The soldiers standing behind Lane congratulated each other. Lane grabbed Manteo by the wrist and led him up to Menatonan. What they did not know was that the chief was lame and could not walk.

"Tell this heathen that he will pay tribute to me at Roanoke and serve the Lord Jesus or all of his people will die!" Manteo interpreted for Lane with a shaky voice. Lane wondered how Menatonan knew he was coming and what his intentions were. Menatonan hesitated to say anything as he stared at the dead bodies of some of his warriors in the grass only yards from where he sat. Behind Menatonan, dressed in fancy buckskins that had been dyed red and white, was Skico, Menatonan's oldest son. Skico stood tall with his arms crossed and looked at Lane like he wanted to tear his head off. Irritated, Lane pointed to the young Skico and told his men to shoot him. Menatonan shouted that it was his son and Manteo quickly told Lane that Menatonan agreed to his demands.

"Hold your fire," Lane quietly said. Skico did not flinch as he looked at the barrel of a gun that was pointed directly at him.

"Who is this?" Lane asked Manteo as he pointed to Skico. Manteo told Lane the truth. Lane ordered that Skico be sent back to Roanoke on the ship as a prisoner. Skico departed without resistance and told his father to notify the fierce Mandoags as he was loaded onto the ship.

Lane spent the next hour talking to Menatonan through Manteo. Menatonan did agree to pay tribute. He even gave Lane the very pearl necklace he had on around his neck. Lane wanted to know the source of the pearls. Menatonan directed Lane to another chiefdom, where modern day Carney Island, Virginia is today. He told a tale of huge white pearls that could be found there. Lane continued to grill Menatonan as to the location of other resources. He pulled out a gold coin.

"Ask him if he has ever seen this type of metal." Lane's eyes grew as Menatonan gave his answer while nodding his head yes. Menatonan sent Lane deep into the Mandoag country with tales of a river that came out a rock that contained lots of wassador. Wassador was the name the Natives of many Eastern North Carolina tribes used for all metals though, so Lane asked about the color and hardness. Menatonan replied that it was softer than the shells the English were wearing and not as red as the copper they had. Lane started to get gold fever. He ordered the ship back to Roanoke with Amadas, Skico and ten men but decided to press on in two large longboats with the rest of the soldiers and Manteo to the destination Menatonan mentioned. This destination was called Temoatan and was the home of the Mandoag chief Okisko. Lane also learned from Menatonan that Wingina was the one who had warned the Chowanoke people of his coming. Lane decided he would deal with Wingina as soon as he returned. All he could think about now was gold.

Lane's lust for gold was so great that he forgot to procure food from the village of Chowanoke and immediately headed further up the river in all haste. Again, no Natives were in sight and every village the English stopped at had been stripped bare and abandoned. The men were thrilled at their victory and the prospect of gold. By nightfall, they realized that they only had one more day of rations left. The men did not want to return without the gold and voted to press on. They even decided to eat two hunting dogs they had with them and season them with sassafras leaves in a stew so that they could continue on for another two days.

The soldiers camped on the bank of the river that night and finally saw some signs of life. In the distance, they saw several camp fires that looked to be reachable in the morning. More than anything, Manteo just wanted to go home.

In the morning, a fog set in. Due to a complete lack of wind, the two longboats had to use oars instead of sails. Out of the fog, the Englishmen heard native voices and thought they were calling to Manteo. The voices broke into an eerie song that caused Manteo to take cover in the bottom of the boat. Manteo cried out that the Mandoag were there and wished to fight. The moment Manteo said this, the song ended with a screech of dozens of voices all hollering and arrows began to rain down on the boats from both sides of the riverbank, which was very narrow and steep. Luckily for the English, and probably due to the fog, no one was hurt, but everyone's heart rates were up and the men clutched their guns.

A few men fired their guns blindly into the woods. The men landed and immediately got in formation with long spears and armor. The soldiers rushed into the woods and found no one. They searched for a while but found no trace, not one footprint. The Mandoag lived up to their name. They were indeed stealthy and fierce. The soldiers returned to the boats and suddenly had a change of heart. They were out of food and had already eaten the dogs. Another vote was held, and everyone agreed to return to Roanoke. Manteo began to feel like a prisoner. He still liked Harriot and he had loved England, but he hated Ralph Lane.

On the voyage back to Roanoke, the soldiers had to fast for two days. On their third day, they stumbled upon some fish caught in an abandoned weir net at yet another abandoned town. They were so ecstatic at their find that many of the men ravenously took bites of the raw fish after scaling them.

When they finally reached Roanoke Island, they ate like the pigs they were and slept.

The following quotes are from Ralph Lane's report:

"I tooke a resolution with my selfe, having dismissed Menatonon upon a ransome agreed for, and sent his sonne into the Pinnesse to Roanoak,"

"In the evening whereof, about three of the clocke wee heard certaine Savages call as we thought, Manteo, who was also at that time with me in the boat, whereof we all being very glad, hoping of some friendly conference with them, and making him to answere them, they presently began a song, as we thought, in token of our welcome to them: but Manteo presently betooke him to his piece, and tolde mee that they meant to fight with us: which worde was not so soone spoken by him, and the light horseman ready to put to shoare, but there lighted a vollie of their arrowes amongst them in the boat, but did no hurt (God be thanked) to any man. Immediately, the other boate lying ready with their shot to skoure the place for our hand weapons to lande upon, which was presently done, although the land was very high and steepe, the Savages forthwith quitted the shoare, and betooke themselves to flight: wee landed, and having faire and easily followed for a smal time after them, who had wooded themselves we know not where:"

'The ende was, we came the next day by night to the Rivers mouth within foure or five miles of the same, having rowed in one day downe the current, as much as in foure dayes wee had done against the same: we lodged upon an Iland, where we had nothing in the world to eate but pottage of Sassafras leaves, the like whereof for a meate was never used before as I thinke. The broad sound wee had to passe the next day all fresh and fasting: that day the winde blew so strongly, and the billow so great, that there was no possibilitie of passage without sinking of our boates. This was upon Easter eve, which was fasted very truely. Upon Easter day in the morning the winde comming very calme,

we entred the sound, and by foure of the clocke we were at Chipanum, whence all the Savages that we had left there were fled, but their wears did yeelde us some fish, as God was pleased not utterly to suffer us to be lost: for some of our company of the light horsemen were farre spent."

"For Pemisapan, who had changed his name of Wingina upon the death of his brother Granganimo, had given both the Choanists, and Mangoaks worde of my purpose touching them, I having bene inforced to make him privie to the same, to bee served by him of a guide to the Mangoaks,"

"And true it was that at that time the assembly was holden at Chawanook about us, as I found at my coming thither, which being unlooked for did so dismay them, as it made us have the better hand at them. But this confederacie against us of the Choanists and Mangoaks was altogether and wholly procured by Pemisapan him-selfe, as Menatonon confessed unto me, who sent them continual word, that our purpose was fully bent to destroy them: on the other side he told me, that they had the like meaning towards us. Hee in the like sort having sent word to the Mangoaks of mine intention to passe up into their River, and to kill them (as he saide) both they and the Moratoks, with whom before wee were entred into a league, and they had ever dealt kindly with us, abandoned their Townes along the River, and retired themselves with their Crenepos, and their Corne within the maine: insomuch as having passed three dayes voyage up the River, wee could not meete a man, nor finde a graine of Corne in any their Townes: whereupon considering with my selfe that wee had but two dayes victuall left, and that wee were then 160. miles from home, besides casualtie of contrary windes or stormes, and suspecting treason of our owne Savages in the discoverie of our voyage intended,"

Invisible Arrows

While Ralph Lane and his men were gone, Wingina had stopped paying his required daily tribute. He had heard false reports from the Mandoag that all the English with Lane had been killed. Wingina had become bolder and started to send raids at night to tear up the English fishing nets. Wingina's plan was to starve the English so that they would spread out to look for food. Once they were spread out, he and the Mandoag together would attack and clear Roanoke Island of the English. His plan was working. The English on Roanoke Island were beginning to starve. The news that Lane and his men lived mattered not to Wingina. He wanted them all gone.

Wingina's brother, Granganimeo, had died of an English disease as had almost a hundred others from his tribe. Upon this death Wingina changed his name to Pemisapan. In addition, Wingina was being pressured by his father Ensenore to be allies with the English again. Ensenore believed that the English were more harmful dead than when alive. He thought all the death due to disease came from English ghosts slaughtering the native men by draining their strength until they died.

To make matters worse, a group of twenty messengers had been sent from Menatonan to Roanoke. Menatonan wanted his son Skico released and told the messengers to tell Lane that not only was he paying tribute but he had convinced Okisko of the Mandoag to surrender and pay tribute. Manteo got word of this to Wingina on a trip to the mainland with Harriot. Without the support of the Mandoag, Wingina knew he could not defeat the English.

Wingina grudgingly sent over a large tribute of grain to Ralph Lane. The English were happy and began to trade axes and copper with Wingina's people again. Wingina even had his men repair the fishing weirs that had been destroyed and gave them land on the mainland to plant their own grain. Wingina hoped this would stop the invisible arrows that plagued his people.

All was well, until Ensenore took ill and died. This made no sense to Wingina, for Ensenore was the one who had pushed him to make amends with the English. Wingina's rage came back and so did someone else who was very familiar with the English. It was Wanchese. Wanchese explained to Wingina that the English were not ghosts and that in England the land was full of disease that struck down many English men, especially children. He confidently told Wingina that denying the English food was the best way to get them to leave. Even Manteo had said upon arrival from England that the English were not a people of the land and they would have to depend on the natives for food. Wanchese also convinced the Mandoag that the English could be defeated and once again, the plan of starving the English and then attacking them was adopted.

A month long series of ceremonies were held to honor Ensenore. Wingina ordered his people to stop going to Roanoke to trade, and thus the English began to run out of food again. Menatonan still sent tributes in hopes that Skico would be released. He even offered a huge string of pearls as ransom for his son's freedom. Lane refused this offer and sent it back.

Wingina sent his best warrior, Osacan, to try and help Skico escape. He thought that if he freed Menatonan's son, it would get the Chowanokes on his side. Wingina figured that Menatonan was only friendly to the English because he did not want his son to be killed. Even if the Chowanoke did not join Wingina in battle, the English would starve faster without Menatonan's tributes.

Osacan snuck over to Roanoke by canoe at night and managed to get to the settlement undetected. After sneaking around in the dark, Osacan located the house containing Skico. He found it because he could hear Skico talking in his native language to someone. Osacan peered in through a window and saw Skico and Manteo both in shackles sitting on the dirt floor by a candle.

Lane did not trust Manteo, who he knew wanted to go home to Croatoan. After all, Manteo was hungry too and had a home in reach to go to. The door to the house Manteo and Skico were in was locked from the outside. Osacan was attempting to open the door when an English voice cried out. Osacan fled into the woods and did not look back. He could hear many voices shouting and dogs barking. His heart raced as he plowed through heavy beds of reeds and sunk up to his shins in the marshy ground.

Osacan escaped to his canoe and headed straight for Wingina on the mainland opposite Roanoke. Once there, he explained that Manteo was no longer a guest of the English but a prisoner. This news made Wingina grin. He thanked Osacan and sat down to smoke a pipe. By Wingina's side sat Wanchese. The two men talked in privacy.

In the morning, Lane heard about the attempted jail break and decided to let Skico go. Lane did not want to anger the only tribe left that was bringing them food. Skico spent a night on the mainland opposite Roanoke on his journey home to Chowanoke. Here, Wingina met him. Wingina assumed Skico also hated the English. Wingina told Skico of his plans to get rid of the English, and he attempted to get Skico to persuade Menatonan to join in the attacks, once the English spread out to find food.

However, Skico had been told by Lane that it was Wingina's fault that the Chowanoke were attacked by the English. Lane had lied to Skico saying that Wingina told him the Chowanoke were raising an army to come and destroy the English and that is why the English attacked first. Skico believed this lie since he was after all released and was not ill treated by the English while held captive on Roanoke. Lane went on to tell Skico that he had only held him so long because they were starving and needed to be sure someone would send tribute. Skico said he knew the English and Chowanoke would be friends once Skico explained everything to his father. Skico went straight home and told Menatonan about Wingina. Menatonan was overjoyed to see his son home and wept tears of joy when he saw him. Menatonan listened to Skico retell Lane's lies and of Wingina's plot to kill the English. Immediately, Menatonan sent word to Lane of Wingina's plans.

By the time this news reached Lane, his men were already somewhat spread out. Wingina's plan was working. Lane had sent Captain Stafford with twenty men to Croatoan to live and hunt for deer and oysters. Stafford was also told to watch for supply ships that were long overdue. Manteo's people at Croatoan were still on friendly terms with the English and allowed this. Another ten men had been sent to Hatorask to live off the land there. This reduced the number of men at Roanoke by about a third.

Lane was taking no chances. He was in a state of near panic. His men were spread out and hungry. None had died yet but many were weak. He asked Menatonan for any warriors he could spare and sent over some tin pots and a mirror. Lane also moved Manteo into his own house and ordered guards posted around the settlement at all hours. Lane did not want Wingina to know that he knew they were enemies again and came up with a wild plot to kill Wingina through trickery.

More quotes from Ralph Lane:

"Within certaine dayes after my returne from the sayd journey, Menatonon sent a messenger to visite his sonne the prisoner with me, and sent me certaine pearle for

a present, or rather, as Pemisapan tolde mee, for the ransome of his sonne, and therefore I refused them:"

"Ensenore a Savage father to Pemisapan being the onely friend to our nation that we had amongst them, and about the King, died the 20 of April 1586. He alone had before opposed himselfe in their consultations against all matters proposed against us, which both the King and all the rest of them after Grangemoes death, were very willing to have preferred. And he was not onely by the meere providence of God during his life, a meane to save us from hurt, as poysonings and such like, but also to doe us very great good, and singularly in this."

"In mine absence on my voyage that I had made against the Chaonists, and Mangoaks, they had raised a brute among themselves, that I and my company were part slaine, and part starved by the Chaonists, and Mangoaks. One part of this tale was too true, that I and mine were like to be starved, but the other false."

"But even in the beginning of this bruite I returned, which when hee sawe contrary to his expectation, and the advertisement that hee had received: that not onely my selfe, and my company were all safe, but also by report of his owne 3. Savages which had bene with mee besides Manteo in that voyage, that is to say, Tetepano, his sisters husband Eracano, and Cossine, that the Chanoists and Mangoaks (whose name and multitude besides their valour is terrible to all the rest of the provinces) durst not for the most part of them abide us, and that those that did abide us were killed, and that we had taken Menatonon prisoner, and brought his sonne that he best loved to Roanoak with mee, it did not a little asswage all devises against us: on the other side, it made Ensenores opinions to bee received againe with greater respects. For he had often before tolde them, and then renewed those his former speeches, both to the king and

the rest, that wee were the servants of God, and that wee were not subject to bee destroyed by them: but contrarywise, that they amongst them that sought our destruction, should finde their owne, and not bee able to worke ours, and that we being dead men were able to doe them more hurt, then now we could do being alive: an opinion very confidently at this day holden by the wisest amongst them, and of their old men, as also, that they have bene in the night, being 100. miles from any of us, in the aire shot at, and stroken by some men of ours, that by sicknesse had died among them: and many of them holde opinion, that we be dead men returned into the world againe, and that wee doe not remaine dead but for a certaine time, and that then we returne againe."

"All which being done, and acknowledged by them all, in the presence of Pemisapan his father, and all his Savages in counsell then with him, it did for the time thorowly (as it seemed) change him in disposition toward us: Insomuch as foorthwith Ensenore wanne this resolution of him, that out of hand he should goe about, and withall, to cause his men to set up wears foorthwith for us: both which he at that present went in hande withall, and did so labour the expedition of it, that in the end of April he had sowed a good quantitie of ground, so much as had bene sufficient, to have fed our whole company"

"For within few dayes after, as before is saide, En-senore our friend died, who was no sooner dead, but certaine of our great enemies about Pemisapan, as Osacan a Werowance, Tanaquiny and Wanchese most principally, were in hand againe to put their old practises in use against us, which were readily imbraced, and all their former devises against us reneued,"

"they agreed and did immediately put it in practise, that they should not for any copper sell us any victuals whatsoever: besides that in the night they should sende to

*have our wears robbed, and also to cause them to bee
broken, and once being broken never to be repaired againe
by them."*

*"For the famine grew so extreeme among us, or
weares failing us of fish, that I was enforced to sende
Captaine Stafford with 20. with him to Croatoan my Lord
Admirals Iland to serve two turnes in one, that is to say, to
feede himselfe and his company, and also to keepe watch if
any shipping came upon the coast to warne us of the same. I
sent M. Pridiox with the pinnesse to Hatorask, and ten with
him, with the Provost Marshal to live there, and also to wait
for shipping: also I sent every weeke 16. or 20. of the rest of
the company to the maine over against us, to live of Casada
and oysters."*

It is probably a lie that Skico had all of Wingina's
plans revealed to him and then told Lane of Wingina's plan.
Lane states in his narrative that Skico, his prisoner,
attempted to run away once and was beaten for it. Lane then
says that he threatened to cut the boy's head off if he tried to
leave again. So, Lane tries to say that Skico, who has seen
his village attacked, his father forced to pay ransom, and has
been held prisoner by Lane and apparently beaten and
threatened with beheading for trying to escape, has shared
with him Wingina's plot to kill the English. Clearly Lane
lied to excuse his actions against Wingina/Pemisapan which
you will learn of next.

More quotes from Lane:

*"The day of their assembly aforesaid at Roanoak was
appointed the 10. of June: all which the premises were
discovered by Skyco, the King Menatonon his sonne my
prisoner, who having once attempted to run away, I laid him
in the bylboes, threatning to cut off his head, whom I
remitted at Pemisapans request: whereupon hee being
perswaded that hee was our enemie to the death, he did not*

onely feed him with himselfe, but also made him acquainted with all his practises. On the other side, the yong man finding himselfe as well used at my hande, as I had meanes to shew, and that all my company made much of him, he flatly discovered al unto me,"

Famine to Feast

Captain Stafford and 10 men sat in a green and white long boat with a limp sail mesmerized by what they heard and saw ahead. They rowed slowly and quietly across the slick as glass surface of the Pamilco Sound. A few yards behind them Master Kendall and 10 more men, including ·Marmaduke and Roger, sat in an unpainted longboat transfixed at the sight ahead of Stafford's boat. They were about 500 yards North from Croatoan and could hear the rhythmic, deep bass tones of drums and loud chanting and singing. They could see the tiny wooded ridge and dozens of distant flickering lights from the many fires strung out across the ridge. The Pamlico had trails of orange, yellow and red dancing across it from the setting sun. The men in the long boats paid no attention to the beautiful sunset off the starboard bow. They were nervous and excited. Was this a dream? The buzzing chirp of cicadas and crickets and the harsh honking of the great herring filled the men's ears but the man-made sounds were what alarmed them. The drums and singing sounded like thousands of voices and indeed it was. Manteo was not with the Englishmen to help them communicate but the Croatoan tribe had always been friendly to the English before. What was the occasion for such celebration, the men wondered.

A great point of land jetted out from Croatoan into the sound and unlike the rest of the island was not covered in woods. It was a grassy point nearly a mile long and covered with people dancing and a fire at least 15 feet tall in the middle. By the time the English rowed all the way to shore, it was dark. They anchored in less than a foot of water about

30 yards from shore as the boats began to scrape bottom. The beach on the sound side of Croatoan was covered in roots and white scallop shells. Indeed the forest ran right down the ridge into the sound. Tree stumps were common as far as 100 yards out from the shore. Immediately, the thin, grey sand beach gave way to a slight incline covered with live oaks, cedars and gum trees but pine dominated most of the forest. The ridge gently rose about 35 feet above sea level and on the other side of this ridge as well as on top of it were hundreds of houses. The homes are scattered like a string of broken pearls and look like all the other homes seen in this new world so far. Sapling poles and reeds covered in birch bark with fire pits outside. The light wind does circles in the fire pits throwing up tiny, white ash tornadoes. Everywhere are heaps of shells and fields of corn, squash and beans.

Four men are left with the boats while Stafford and 16 others climb the ridge to the town. No one seems to be around. They can tell the drums are now consolidated to the West. Master Kendal fiddles with a gold ring on his finger and looks down at the lion seal on it. If things get bad I can trade this for almost anything he thought. Suddenly all of the loud drumming and singing stopped and all fires went out aside from the big one. It was an eerie quiet broken only by the call of an owl. Kendal is startled by a hand on his shoulder and an old woman shouting, 'Pyas!' which means 'come here.' Kendal dropped the ring and turned to see the woman smiling. Kendal bent down to pick up the ring but could not find it. It was dark out now and the trees shaded the moon light to a dim glow. He searched frantically but found he was being left as Stafford and the others began to follow the woman down a well-worn path through the woods. Kendal kept searching until his fellows were out of sight then hurried along after them without his ring.

As they started down the path they saw more and more people on the path heading the same direction. Stafford was startled to see a young mother walking while breast feeding a baby. The old woman led the English to a felled log out on the grassy point where over a thousand had gathered around a huge fire shaking rattles and beating drums. Someone with many necklaces and skins on and a copper crown was speaking to the crowd.

"Apis," said the old woman softly which means 'sit down.' Stafford and his men quietly sat down and were stared at by all around them. Stafford knew better than to interrupt whatever was going on by starting to trade the goods they had brought with them. The men sat and watched not knowing a word that was said.

Stafford guessed by the time of year and the full moon that the festival probably had something to do with the coming of harvest time. He had learned from Manteo that the year was divided into 13 months by the thirteen full moons in a year. The English were soon handed cooked fish and venison, which being half starved from their time on Roanoke, they devoured. The speaker seemed to be finished and a general party ensued. The copper crown speaker walked over to the English with a huge smile and Stafford stood and handed him a fine axe. Perhaps with Granganimeo dead, this was a celebration of a new leader. Whatever was going on the men were happy to be fed a good meal.

Back on the longboats, the four men swatted mosquitoes. They were eager for their friends to return and tell them they could set up camp. Any duty was better than being under the eye of Ralph Lane. He nearly worked the men to death building houses and other structures on Roanoke Island. Very few natives ever went to Roanoke to trade thanks to Lane's ignorance and cruelty and thus the starvation had begun. They were lucky to be free of it and go to a land yet unmolested by Lane. Barlowe had a good relationship with the people of this island the year before, and for the first month of the 1585 arrival most of the men had again lived on Croatoan while awaiting the arrival of the flag ship Tiger.

Just as the men in the longboats began to negotiate who would stand watch while the rest of them slept Stafford returned with the other 16 men and about a dozen Croatoan men. Together they drug the longboats to shore through a slightly deeper channel not known to the English (Cape Creek). They passed by a labyrinth of weir nets and could see hundreds of fish trapped inside swimming and splashing as the trample of the men's feet through the shallow water startled them.

"It is going to be much easier here. We have the aid of a village so long as we do not mistreat them. We need to find our way to the ocean side of the island in the morning to begin watch for our fleet or that of the Spanish." Stafford sounded relieved. The men would set up camp on the eastern edge of the main town on Croatoan. This way they were close enough to see the ocean by climbing a ladder at the top of the hill to see over the trees. They could look for approaching fleets as ordered by Lane and be close enough to the Croatoan to receive food and trade. They stayed together and kept a keen eye to the sea. This would be the first but not the last time Captain Stafford left Roanoke for Croatoan....

Heads Roll

Manteo at this time became a prisoner. Lane needed Manteo and he knew it. Wingina knew this too. Wingina wanted to try and free Manteo. Not only would this rob Lane of his means of communicating with Menatonan, but it would also give Wingina the inside scoop on the English. No one knew the English and their situation better than Manteo. Once again, Wingina turned to Osacan. Osacan said that he wasted a lot of time on his trip to try to free Skico looking for the right building. Now that he knew which building to go to, he felt it would be easy, especially since there were no guards. The weather was favorable too. It was cloudy and if this held into the night it would be completely dark. Wingina sent three others with Osacan this time to watch each others backs.

Lane told his men to allow any Indians that came over to land their canoes.

"Let them come over but do not let them leave. If they come to trade, let them but if they persist in leaving, kill them." Lane addressed his men in front of the little fort on the northwest end of Roanoke Island with all his armor on, even the helmet.

"I do not want Wingina to know that I know his plans to wipe us out. It will be easier to kill him if he comes here to this Island, for we can set up an ambush. If we must go to the mainland and attack, it will be much more difficult. I want him to think his plan is working and that we are all spread out as he hopes. If any of his people come over to trade, assume they are really just spies. If these spies return and say we still have around 70 men on the island, they will not attack, for they know they can starve us further until we are forced to send more men to Croatoan and Hatorask."

As Lane spoke, Osacan and his three companions were spotted by a look out.

"Master Lane, a canoe approaches! Four savages and they do have bows with them." The lookout, a carpenter named Thomas, searched the sound for more canoes and saw none.

When Osacan and the others landed on the shore and crept through the reeds to the settlement, they were quite shocked to see the English waiting for them. As the Indians emerged from the marshy grasses into the woods, they saw about thirty Englishmen with swords waiting for them. Instantly they fled back to their canoe and began to make for the mainland.

However, this was anticipated by Lane who had ordered Captain Reynolds in the light boat to cut them off. The light boat rammed the little canoe, which had made it about 2/3 of the way back to the mainland. The Indians leaped out of the canoe before it was hit. The sound was only about three feet deep so Osacan and the others stood up and attempted to run. They had barely shaken the water from their faces when the swords came crashing down. The English cut off their heads and returned to Roanoke. The blood rolled through the water like red squid ink forming great expanding clouds and the canoe was left to drift. It was no use trying to hide the bodies. A group of Indians on the shore of the mainland had watched the entire scene in horror.

When the light boat returned, Lane shook off the news with little concern.

"It matters not; we will go in the morning to the mainland and use Manteo as bait to trap and kill their leader."

Just before dawn, Lane took his soldiers including the warriors Menatonan had sent and Manteo to the mainland. He ordered his men to hide in the high reeds near the shore while he took Manteo and the other Indians further into the shore. He told the soldiers that when he gave the signal 'Christ our victor,' they should all rise up and attack.

Lane sent word to Wingina that he wished to complain about Osocan and that he was leaving for Croatoan.

Lane did not have to wait long. Wingina came down to see Lane, along with seven other muscular native men. Behind them were twelve more warriors, including Wanchese but all were unarmed. Wingina was intimidating looking. He was very fit and was painted up like a warrior. Lane smiled upon seeing him and shouted his command signal as loud as he could.

"Christ our victor!!!"

One of the men with Lane shot Wingina in the back with a pistol as the English emerged from the reeds all screaming and shooting.

Wingina was enraged as he fell to the ground. He growled as he stood back up and ran for the woods. Men were fighting all around him and cries of death and agony were heard between the murderous roars of the English guns. An Irish soldier shot Wingina in the butt. Again, Wingina fell, only to rise again and keep running into the woods. Another Irishman followed and Lane thought for sure this man would never return. A moment later, the Irishman came out of the woods holding Wingina's head. The rest of the Indians fled in terror.

Luckily for Lane, the Mandoags had not yet arrived. They had a force of over 700 men and a reputation amongst the natives as being extremely fierce in battle.

During the battle, only one Englishman was slightly wounded when hit in the face by a rock thrown by Wanchese.

The following excerpts are from Lane:

"He (Mater of the light horsemen) met with a Canoa going from the shore, and overthrew the Canoa, and cut off two Savages heads: this was not done so secretly but he was discovered from the shore; wherupon the cry arose: for in

trueth they, privy to their owne villanous purposes against us, held as good espiall upon us, both day and night, as we did upon them."

"I went to Dasamonquepeio: and being landed, sent Pemisapan word by one of his owne Savages that met me at the shore, that I was going to Croatoan, and meant to take him in the way to complaine unto him of Osocon, who the night past was conveying away my prisoner, whom I had there present tied in an handlocke. Heereupon the king did abide my coming to him, and finding my selfe amidst seven or eight of his principall Weroances and followers, (not regarding any of the common sort) I gave the watch-word agreed upon, (which was, Christ our victory) and immediately those his chiefe men and himselfe had by the mercy of God for our deliverance, that which they had purposed for us. The king himselfe being shot thorow by the Colonell with a pistoll, lying on the ground for dead, & I looking as watchfully for the saving of Manteos friends, as others were busie that none of the rest should escape, suddenly he started up, and ran away as though he had not bene touched, insomuch as he overran all the company, being by the way shot thwart the buttocks by mine Irish boy with my petronell. In the end an Irish man serving me, one Nugent, and the deputy provost, undertooke him; and following him in the woods, overtooke him: and I in some doubt least we had lost both the king & my man by our owne negligence to have beene intercepted by the Savages, wee met him returning out of the woods with Pemisapans head in his hand."

For those waiting for Ralph Lane to suffer a horrid death, I am sorry to report he died an old man. He was wounded in Ireland (a place he ravaged even more than the New World) and died of complications from that wound years later. Let us hope he lived in agony those last few years.

Drake

~June 1586~

While Lane was off killing Wingina, his detachment of men on Croatoan stood gripped with a mixture of fear and excitement on the ocean side of the island. A great fleet of twenty-three ships was approaching.

"Do you think they are Spanish?" Marmaduke asked Rodger.

"If they are, we are as good as dead. That fleet is massive." Rodger stared at the horizon and tried to make out the flags of the ships. Soon enough it was revealed that they were English ships. The men on the beach threw their hats in the air and cheered. It was Sir Francis Drake. At once, Captain Stafford sprinted for a longboat to notify Lane that an English fleet had arrived. He traveled all day and night to Roanoke without stopping. They would go home after all. Perhaps Lane would admit that his mishandling of the local affairs with the Indians had led to the failure of the colony and they could all go home.

Captain Stafford found Lane sharpening a battle axe on a grinding wheel on Roanoke Island.

"Sir I have urgent news. Drake's fleet has been spotted off of Croatoan. I left the men there with orders to light fires on the beach to signal our location to the fleet." Stafford panted as he spoke for he had truly made a mad dash for Roanoke. The sight of the fleet had energized his weary spirit. Lane praised God and began to sharpen the axe more vigorously.

"Now we have the means to really show those heathens who their master is!" Lane sunk the axe into a tree stump and ran into his house followed by Stafford. Lane began to write a request of supplies he wanted from Drake that included the use of a shallow draft ship.

"Take this to Drake and explain to him that I wish to move the settlement north to a deeper harbor which contains better pearls. From there, we can build another series of forts that protect our path inland to where the gold is rumored to be." Stafford took the letter and departed for Croatoan at once. To his relief, he did not have to travel that far because Drake was anchored off Hatorask.

Drake had already unloaded some much needed food and casks of water. The settlers ate like the nearly starved men they were and thanked Drake profusely. When Stafford arrived and delivered Lane's message, Drake laughed.

"I can grant you everything on this list and then some. We are fresh off sacking St. Augustine and very well supplied. We stole everything, down to the door hinges from the Spanish. I will leave the bark *Francis* with you, loaded with everything you need. I will also leave you my two best Captains, Abraham Kendall and Griffith Herne." Drake wrote down his response and gave it to Stafford. In Drake's response, he also agreed to take home those of Lane's force that were weak and replace them with able-bodied men from his own fleet.

Lane thanked God when he read Drake's letter and his mind immediately turned to thoughts of further conquest and riches. The ocean spirits were angry though. The ever-hungry belly of the Outer Banks could smell all the fine timber on her waters and wanted to swallow the ships whole. For four days, it blew Northeast and Drake's ships took a beating. The *Francis* was lost, along with her two Captains, Kendall and Herne. Lane's dreams of using the extra men and ships for further conquest of the Indians died.

It was decided that the best course of action would be to head home to England with Drake. The men quickly gathered their things and headed back to England, including Manteo.

As Lane took a longboat through the sound to meet the ships anchored off Hatorask, Mother Ocean decided to punish him further. A wave swept over the boat he was on and stole two chests full of pearls, including the necklace Menatonan had given him. Lane watched in horror as the chests sank leaving nothing but a trail of bubbles.

On the voyage back to England, an old sailor and poet named Randal summed up the 1585 affairs in a song. Luckily for Randal he was not aboard the same ship as Ralph Lane for the trip home. (Not really I wrote this).

"Well, we sailed from East to West,
with a sword and a harquebus.
We came to rob the Spanish of their gold!
Hit a storm off Portugal,
furled the sails and rode the hull.
The wind whipped hard and the water was so cold!
We put in at Puerto Rico and stole two Spanish ships,
little did we know that was as good as it gets.
For as soon as we reached the New World, that's when things went wrong.
We came to a grinding halt at Wokokon.
Now the Indians, they were friendly, fed us and gave
us gifts.
But old Ralph Lane wanted more than he could take!
So he kidnapped the chief's son

and held that boy for ransom,
that's why I thank God for Francis Drake!
He sailed us back to England, got us out of that
awful
mess
and that my friends is our story of sailing from
East to West."

Lane and his men spent almost a year in the New World. Lane blamed the lack of supplies and food as the cause for the failure of the colony. Many others including Grenville blamed Lane's cruelty to the Natives as the reason for the failure of the colony.

Manteo returned to England and would return to the New World less than a year later.

Return of Wanchese

~Summer 1586~

Ironically, the very next day after Lane and his men left Roanoke with Drake, a supply ship, sent by Sir Walter Raleigh, arrived. They were late in arriving because they had been delayed by the very same storm that sank the Francis and swiped Lane's chests of pearls. When they arrived at Roanoke, they saw no one and headed home.

Two weeks after Raleigh's supply ship left, Grenville returned to Roanoke with three ships laden with supplies.

Grenville had been very successful against the Spanish between voyages. When he left the New World back in 1585 on board the *Tiger*; he captured a Spanish galleon full of silver. This ship made Grenville enough money to pay off the entire cost of the 1585 voyage and then some.

When Grenville returned to the New World, he was dumbfounded. He landed at Hatorask and saw no signs of any of the men. He looked at Roanoke as well and found it abandoned. He did not want to lose the land they had held for such a long time, so he decided to leave fifteen men on Roanoke Island with enough supplies to last them for two years. They were to live in the houses left behind by the departed settlement and garrison the little fort there.

Grenville left and headed toward the Spanish-held Azores. He was very successful in his raids of the Azores, capturing much booty, which he knew would please Queen Elizabeth.

Back in Roanoke, the fifteen men were about to pay for the mistakes Lane and his soldiers had made. Word spread quickly amongst the Natives that more white men had returned. Wingina was dead, as well as his father Ensenore and his brother Granganimeo. The tribe was left with hundreds dead from disease, a village burned, and a murdered chief. The Natives wanted revenge and needed a fierce leader to take it. Wanchese was just the man to do this, as he was not afraid of the English.

Wanchese waited until all of the English ships were gone before he acted. Shortly after the English ships left, Wanchese held a gathering of the Native warriors from Secotan, Aquscogoc, and Dasamonquepeu, towns from Wingina's old chiefdom. This meeting was held on the mainland opposite Roanoke Island. Standing up on a large cypress stump, Wanchese spoke to the crowd of warriors.

"We will go to the island of Roanoke and position ourselves in the high reeds around the English houses. I will call out to them in their own tongue. Once they are out in the open we will spill their blood with clubs and arrows. If they flee to one of the houses we will have torches ready to burn them out. Let us go and conceal ourselves at night while they sleep. I will approach them tomorrow morning and we will rid our land of these terrible people."

That night, the men stood in a circle around a fire with armor made from reeds covering their chests. They shook rattles made of gourds and beat drums of wood and hides. Two women walked around each carrying a bowl full of crushed berries and roots that made dyes. The warriors dipped their fingers into the bowls and painted their faces black and red for battle and selected their best arrows for the upcoming fight.

Once painted up and well armed, the warriors formed a circle around the fire and all looked at Wanchese. Wanchese held up a large whelk shell cup full of Yaupon tea above his head with both hands. The drums and rattles stopped and there was a long silence. All that could be heard was the buzz of the crickets and the croak of frogs. The cool night air was full of stars and the half moon had a slight green tent. Wanchese held the shell high and looked to his left and his right at the warriors gathered around the fire.

"My brothers, these pale invaders have killed our beloved Wingina. They have brought an incurable and terrible plague to our villages and stolen or destroyed many of our crops. We have tried to be friendly and treated the visitors as we treat each other. The pale faces do not see us as brothers of the Earth. They think we are inferior and beneath them. Their hearts and minds are closed to our suffering which they have caused. It is time now to fight and rid the land of these monsters!"

The crowd of warriors shook their gourds and cheered. Wanchese then passed the shell cup to the man on his right and pounded his own reed armor with his fists. Each man drank from the shell and then passed it to the man next to him. Wanchese drank last to the hooting of his men and the steady beat of the drums. After he finished off the cup he threw the shell down and smashed it with his war club. The warriors began to whoop and holler even louder as they stomped around the fire and beat their chests.

At dawn, after having purged themselves with yaupon tea, they left for Roanoke Island by canoes. The men were full of energy and hatred, ready for battle. Once on Roanoke, they quietly pulled their canoes to shore and headed to the houses near the fort. They hid in the high reeds near the houses and waited for Wanchese to draw the English out. The English were completely unaware of their angry visitors, and to make matters worse for the English, only eleven of them were present. The other four settlers were in a creek about a quarter of a mile away collecting oysters.

Wanchese told his men to light torches with a burning glass they had received through trade with the English the year before.

"Wait for my signal and be ready to burn them out should they flee into one of the houses. Remember, Tanaquity gets the honor of the first kill, and then we can attack." Wanchese whispered to his men. The men fanned out quietly and knelt down with bows and arrows in hand.

"Hello?, Hello?, Hello!," Wanchese said repeatedly. All eleven Englishmen heard this and were bewildered. They gathered together and went to see who the Indian was speaking to them in English. Wanchese stood next to Tanaquity, who was the brother of the recently murdered Osacan. The rest of the Indians remained hidden. Two of the English stepped forward happy that they might have someone to trade with. Wanchese smiled and held his arms out to show he wanted to hug the Englishman who stood directly in front of him. The Englishman hesitated, but then hugged Wanchese.

Wanchese bear-hugged the man as tight as he could and let out a war cry to signal his men to attack. (Lane had taught them well how best to kill). Tanaquity pulled out a war club he had hidden underneath a bearskin and smashed the skull of the Englishman Wanchese was holding. The man dropped to the pinestraw covered ground with a thud. A river of blood rushed out of his head. The rest of the English fled to the house that contained most of their weapons while dodging a shower of arrows. Before the English could load the guns or put on their armor, the Indians had already thrown torches on the thatch roof of the house, which began to roar with orange and red flames. There was a barrel of gunpowder inside the house, so the English knew they had to come out fighting or be blown to pieces. They grabbed pikes, swords, and shields and lined up at the only door all looking at each other with fear in their eyes.

"This is it men. We come out fighting and beat a retreat to the longboats and the others," John Withers said as he gripped a halberd.

John was the first who man ran out the door, yelling a battle cry and was shot in the face with an arrow. The arrow went into his open mouth and out the back of his neck. His yell immediately ended, he gurgled some blood, and fell over dead. The other nine Englishmen fanned out behind their fallen comrade with a variety of weapons. One man carried a long bow and had wrapped the tip of an arrow with cloth and lit it on fire from the flames of the burning building. He made good use of this arrow by shooting Tanaquity through the thigh with it. The warrior fell to the ground grabbing his leg and was dragged into the woods by Wanchese.

For an hour, the English beat a retreat to the sound where their longboats were kept. The Indians pursued and continued to whoop and holler as they fired arrows and threw spears.

The English made it to their longboats and rowed as fast as they could out to the creek where the other four Englishmen were collecting oysters. Together, the 13 survivors fled Roanoke to Hatorask. Wanchese and his men did not chase them any further. Instead, they took to the task of destroying the little fort on the north end by burning the log walls.

This chapter was based on two sources. The details of the 15 Englishmen being attacked by warriors from the mainland comes from John Whites account of the 1587 voyage. The rest of the chapter is based on a report from Richard Hakluyt on Richard Grenville's return voyage to the New World in 1586 to resupply Ralph Lane's men. He arrived two weeks after Lane's group had departed with Francis Drake.

This first excerpt is from John White:

"We also understood of the men of Croatoan, that our man Master Howe was slaine by the remnant of Winginos men dwelling then at Dasamonguepeuk, with whom Wanchese kept companie: and also we understood by them of Croatoan, how that the 15 Englishmen left at Roanoak the yeere before, by Sir Richard Grinvile, were suddenly set upon, by 30 of the men of Secota, Aquascogoc, and Dasamonguepek, in manner following. They conveyed themselves secretly behind the trees, neere the houses where our men carelesly lived: and having perceived that of those fifteene they could see but eleven only, two of those Savages appeared to the 11 Englishmen, calling to them by friendly signes, that but two of their chiefest men should come unarmed to speake with those two Savages, who seemed also to bee unarmed. Wherefore two of the chiefest of our Englishmen went gladly to them: but whilest one of those Savages traiterously imbraced one of our men, the other with his sworde of wood, which he had secretly hidden under his mantell, strooke him on the head and slew him, and presently the other eight and twenty Savages shewed them selves: the other Englishman perceiving this, fled to his company, whom the Savages pursued with their bowes, and arrowes, so fast, that the Englishmen were forced to take the house, wherein all their victuall, and weapons were: but the Savages, foorthwith set the same on fire: by meanes wherof our men were forced to take up such weapons as came first to hand, and without order to runne foorth among the Savages, with whom they skirmished above an howre. In this skirmish another of our men was shotte into the mouth with an arrow, where hee died: and also one of the Savages was shot into the side by one of our men, with a wild fire arrow, whereof he died presently. The place where they fought was of great advantage to the Savages, by meanes of the thicke trees, behinde which the Savages through their nimblenes, defended themselves, and so offended our men with their

arrowes, that our men being some of them hurt, retyred fighting to the water side, where their boat lay, with which they fled towards Hatorask. By that time they had rowed but a quarter of a mile, they espied their foure fellows coming from a creeke thereby, where they had bene to fetch Oysters: these foure they received into their boate, leaving Roanoak, and landed on a little Island on the right hand of our entrance into the harbour of Hatorask, where they remayned a while, but afterward departed, whither as yet we know not. Having nowe sufficiently dispatched our businesse at Croatoan, the same day we departed friendly, taking our leave, and came aboord the fleete at Hatorask."

These next two excerpts are from Richard Hakluyt about Richard Grenville's 1586 return voyage:

"Immediately after the departing of our English Colony out of this paradise of the world, the ship abovementioned sent and set forth at the charges of Sir Walter Ralegh and his direction, arrived at Hatorask; who after some time spent in seeking our Colony up in the countrey, and not finding them, returned with all the aforesayd provision into England."

"after good deliberation, hee determined to leave some men behinde to reteine possession of the Countrey: whereupon he landed fifteene men in the Isle of Roanoak, furnished plentifully with all maner of provision for two yeeres, and so departed for England. Not long after he fell with the Isles of Açores, on some of which Islands he landed, and spoiled the townes of all such things as were woorth cariage, where also he tooke divers Spanyards. With these and many other exploits done by him in this voyage, aswell outward as homeward, he returned into England."

Never Trust a Pirate

~Spring 1587~

Back in England, it is decided that another attempt to settle the New World will be made. This time they plan to settle near the Chesapeake Bay. They are planning to bring women this time and several wealthy investors. The Chesapeake has a deeper harbor and rumors of larger pearls. John White will be returning, along with his pregnant daughter Eleanor. They plan to stop at Roanoke to pick up the 15 men that Grenville left there, and then head north to Chesapeake Bay. This was their plan, but almost nothing went right on this voyage from the beginning to the end. Simon Fernando, a former pirate, but an excellent pilot was selected to guide the colony to the New World.

The voyage consisted of three ships: the *Lion*, which John White was on, a flyboat commanded by Captain Spicer, and a pinnace commanded by Captain Stafford. Sir Walter Raleigh appointed John White as the governor of the colony and named the new land Virginia, after Queen Elizabeth, the virgin queen.

Once again, Simon Fernando is the ship's pilot for the *Lion*. His actions will prove that he is bent on the failure of the colony.

The journey starts out smoothly, with a historic fare-well from fellow countrymen. The trip is without merit until they reach the waters off Portugal, Fernando's home country.

All three ships are at anchor for the night, when Fernando decides to slip away in the dead of night without telling the flyboat or his sleeping passengers. Captain Stafford, however, sees this action and follows in the pinnace, assuming Captain Spicer on the flyboat must have been informed of a previously agreed upon hour of departure and wondered why he himself had not been informed. This is actually Fernando's first attempt at sabotage.

In the morning, John White decides to take a stroll on deck. He is standing at the stern of the ship, gazing out at the horizon. Manteo is standing next to him, a bit confused.

"Where the devil is the flyboat? Fernando what have you done?" White demanded an explanation for the abandonment of the flyboat. Half of the colonists were on it, as well as most of the supplies for the colony.

"They were right behind us when we left the Bay of Portugal. I went to sleep after that. I am sure we will meet up with them later," Fernando replied with all lack of concern in his voice.

John White was stunned and confused, unable to speak. Manteo only glared at Fernando, remembering what Wanchese had said about Fernando on their first trip to England.

The trip continued on across the Atlantic, with no sign of the flyboat, Captain Spicer, or the missing colonists. Many of the passengers, including John White and Manteo, began to wonder about the real fate of those on board the flyboat. In addition, each day, Simon Fernando began to show a deeper, more hostile side of himself.

Onboard the ship there was definite jealousy between Fernando's sailors and the colonists. Most of the colonists were somewhat wealthy merchants from London, whereas the sailors were poor and from small port towns. While the sailors worked around the clock in four hour shifts, the colonists sat around idle and talked about their hopes for profit and adventure. This made for some tense moments between the two parties on a long journey across mother ocean.

Eventually, the men landed on an island off the coast of Dominica. They were to go on shore and collect fresh water and fruit. Everyone was happy to get off the ship and eat some fruit and drink fresh water. The beer they had been drinking for days on top of days was hot and the heat of the Caribbean was adding to their dehydration.

Fernando guided the colonists to some fruit that looked like small green apples. They hungrily devoured them. Fernando handed one of the fruits to Manteo with a smirk. Manteo shook his head no and gave Fernando a cold stare. Manteo noticed that Fernando had not eaten any of the fruit and knew in his gut that Fernando was up to something.

Moments later a young man began to puke and clutch his stomach. He hit his knees on the black sand beach and vomited again. The others watched in horror as they themselves began to feel the burn inside their chests and a gripping pain fall on their stomachs like a wave. All around Manteo the men and women who ate the fruit began to grab their throats and struggle to breath. Everyone who had eaten the fruit began to vomit and convulse on the beach. Every now and then Manteo could hear a loud wheeze as someone desperately sucked down some air after nearly choking. No one knew if they were all about to die or not. Fernando pretended to share in the misery, but Manteo knew that Fernando had not eaten any of the fruit because he had been watching him closely ever since they had landed.

Manteo looked out to the ship where the sailors were still furling sails and preparing to land. They were watching the colonists struggle and puke but showed no emotion at all.

They looked on as though they were watching a passing cloud.

The colonists became even sicker. The fruit made their mouths and tongues swell up so badly they could not swallow or speak. A baby, who was still nursing, also took ill for his mother had eaten the fruit.

In addition, the water Fernando gave them was also poisoned. It made the eyes of the men who washed their faces in it swell shut so badly that they could not see for five to six days. For five days, these men would sit still inside of the ship in a dark corner while their friends brought them food and beer. Luckily, no one drank this water after seeing how it blinded the first men to splash it on themselves.

The colonists began to see the truth of what was happening here, but had no choice but to keep quiet because they were not sailors, and they needed Fernando and his men to get them to the New World. The colonists began to meet privately and discuss how best to handle the matter, and decided not to let on to what they knew to be happening. They feared if Fernando knew that they were on to him, he would simply kill them all.

The colonists decided to search the island themselves. They found clean water on the other side of a hill next to the beach they had landed on. They caught several huge sea turtles and shot some birds to eat. When Fernando saw this, he immediately began to squawk about it being time to leave and promised he knew of another island where sheep could be found and easily taken. Of course, this proved to be a lie. Fernando simply wasted time by landing on a deserted island that contained nothing but snakes, marsh grass, and a few crabs. Fernando also assured the colonists he would stop for salt so that their meats would not go bad. Once again, he lied.

The most telling thing Fernando did was inform the Irishman, Darby Gland of his plot to abandon the colony at Roanoke rather than take them to the Chesapeake as planned. For when they stopped at Santa Cruz, Darby and another Irishman disappeared from the ship and made their way to the nearest Spanish town. What Darby did was inform the Spanish that the colonists were going to Roanoke. One, how did Darby know the English would be left in Roanoke if this treachery had not already been planned? Two, one can only deduce that Fernando must have instructed Darby to inform the Spanish, in hopes that they would attack England's precious colony. Sadly for Darby Gland, it is unknown what riches may have been promised to him for this obedient act, but his fate actually made him a prisoner of the Spanish for the next seven years.

The following excerpts are from Governor John White:

"The two and twentieth of July wee arrived safe at Hatorask, where our ship and pinnesse ankered: the Governour went aboord the pinnesse, accompanied with fortie of his best men, intending to passe up to Roanoak foorthwith, hoping there to finde those fifteene Englishmen, which Sir Richard Grinvile had left there the yeere before,"

"but as soone as we were put with our pinnesse from the ship, a Gentleman by the meanes of Ferdinando, who was appointed to returne for England, called to the sailers in the pinnesse, charging them not to bring any of the planters backe againe, but to leave them in the Island, except the Governour, & two or three such as he approved, saying that the Summer was farre spent, wherefore hee would land all the planters in no other place."

At Last Hatorask

Finally, on July 22nd the pinnace and the *Lion* reached Hatorask. Manteo was only twenty miles from home at this point and gazed off into the horizon in the direction of his homeland. The sun was setting as Manteo began to daydream, trying to imagine what his friends and relatives back home were doing. The wind was steady from the northeast which meant the sound would be pushed back behind Croatoan village, exposing a muddy bottom full of clams. His mouth began to water for the taste of fresh clams. Manteo figured his brothers were probably filling baskets with clams before dark to boil for dinner. He thought of smiling faces from his village and began to feel waves of excitement roll over him about going home. He was ready for a simpler life again and eager to help his people with English tools and goods.

The colonists were only stopping at Roanoke to pick up the fifteen men Grenville had left there back in 1586. They also wanted to return Manteo to Croatoan and renew the friendly trade relationship they had had in 1584 and 1585. After a few days stop, they were to continue to the Chesapeake to establish a permanent settlement. The waters of the sound were too shallow to bring the *Lion* to Roanoke, so all of the colonists needed to be transferred to the pinnace.

The *Lion* anchored off of Hatorask to transfer all the colonists to the pinnace. The plan was for the colonists to sail to Roanoke while Fernando's sailors took longboats to Hatorask to fill casks with fresh water. The pinnace anchored next to the Lion and boards were placed between the two ships. The colonists on the *Lion* simply walked across these boards carrying their things with them to the pinnace. Fernando's sailors were unusually quiet as they helped transfer supplies to the pinnace.

Once all of the colonists were on board the pinnace and the boards between the ships were pulled up onto the *Lion's* deck, Fernando called out to John White to tell him some shocking news.

"Governor, I am afraid it is too late in the season for me to transport you further. You will have to settle here instead. At least the houses are already built and Manteo's people are nearby. I will allow either you or one of your assistants to sail back with me to England but no more. We have little food and no water, so we will stock up here before returning. Surely you understand." Fernando held on to the shroud lines with one hand as he leaned over the railing and waved with his other arm. The colonists could hear a roar of laughter after they were about 300 yards away in the pinnace.

White said nothing because he knew it was useless. Besides, it would be easier to settle on Roanoke where they had already built around 30 houses and were close enough to trade heavily with the friendly Croatoan. The pinnace passed through the inlet they called Port Fernando and into the sound. The waves heaved the pinnace forward and thrusted her into the sound. The rough ocean gave way to the smooth calm waters of the sound. The sun was straight ahead of the pinnace and looked enormous. It was red and orange and made the surface of the water the same colors. Parallel to the horizon was a line of thin clouds that looked purple under the foot of the sun. Roanoke Island looked black and still. Flat marshes with hundreds of little channels and clumps of pine and other hardwoods led up to the main island of Roanoke.

The *Lion* remained anchored at Hatorask taking on fresh water and wood for recaulking, while Fernando's rough bunch of sailors fished and drank heavily. The rest of the colonist's supplies were hastily unloaded at Hatorask for the pinnace to tote to Roanoke later.

The pinnace pulled into a little harbor on the north end of Roanoke Island near some cliffs. Here the colony landed and began to unload the ship. The air was alive with the buzz of crickets and grass hoppers. Fireflies were everywhere. Tall hardwood tress lined a narrow beach that was no more than five feet wide and was full of twisted roots from the nearby trees. Rose Pain was the first one to hop out of the longboat and onto the sand. This made her the first Englishwoman to set foot in the New World. She was followed by the two pregnant women, Misses Harvie and Misses Dare. No one mentioned anything about the historical significance but Rose made a note of it in her mind.

John White stood with Manteo and addressed the forty-two colonists that had arrived. "My friends, we are already reduced by more than half since Fernando abandoned the flyboat. We must stick together and work hard to make this a pleasant home. We are given a new start, real freedom... and many dangers. The settlement built by our soldiers is a very short walk from here. We should go there immediately before it is completely dark out. There are fifteen soldiers there that can give us news of the natives attitude towards us. Let's not linger. We need to go now while the sun is still up." John White was excited to be back. Perhaps no other Englishmen had looked so carefully at the New World and its beauty as John White had. Through his paintings, it is obvious that John was attempting to pay attention to detail.

However, unbeknownst to them all, the other seventy-five colonists were breaking waves in the flyboat off of Croatoan. The flyboat could see the *Lion* anchored off of Hatorask and were making their way North as fast as the winds would allow. Despite Fernando's efforts to ditch the flyboat at Portugal, her captain got her to her destination safely. He had never been to the New World but found his way with little trouble. The colonists on the flyboat had actually had a pleasant trip over in comparison with the others under Fernando's care.

Manteo led the way as the colonists walked in a line down a deer path that led to the old settlement. By the time they all reached the settlement, it was dark. Martin Sutton, a farmer back in England, held a lantern up as he emerged from the woods to a clearing. The houses were simple squares with wooden frames and sandy clay walls. There was no sight or sound of the fifteen settlers. A few people called out 'hello' but there was no reply. Martin approached a half open door to one of the houses. He hesitated as he approached the door with his hand out shaking. The other colonists watched Martin as he jumped out of the way of a deer that bolted out of the house and nearly ran him over. They all let out a nervous chuckle. Mosquitoes bit the newcomers constantly while paying Manteo no attention.

The houses were overgrown with melons and had deer inside of them eating the melons. They were void of furniture but otherwise had good roofs and sturdy walls.

Manteo was eager to go home to Croatoan once they found Grenville's 15 men.

"If we go to Croatoan, my people can feed us and help build shelters. They will be eager to trade with the English. I have been away from home for too long and need to go back," Manteo said to John White.

"Yes, we will take you home and renew our old friendship with your people but first we must find these men. They are probably at the fort. We can take the pinnace up there in the morning." John had many thoughts on his mind. He knew that someone would have to return to England with Fernando to explain that they had been left at Roanoke. John was furious at Fernando and his sailors but at the same time helpless.

The men and women filed into the houses and began filling bags with pine straw to sleep on. A small fire was built in a fire pit located in the center of the settlement. Manteo and some of the colonists were able to fill three baskets with oysters from the tip of a creek that ran right up to the settlement. These oysters were boiled over the fire as the colonists sat around and looked at the stars. They were happy to be off the rolling ship and to already have procured a feast from the land.

That first night, everyone was excited as they went to sleep in a New World. Manteo closed his eyes and took a deep breath through his nose. Even the smell of the air was familiar. He was close to home and eager to get there. Ananias Dare sat behind his wife inside one of the houses and rubbed her pregnant belly.

"Did you feel that one? The baby just kicked."

"Yes that was a strong kick. It must be a boy," Ananias joked. With thirty houses and only 42 people, couples were given their own house. Manteo chose to sleep on a pile of hay stacked against one of the walls of the Governor's house. He wanted to feel the breeze on his face and take in the fresh air. The stench of the ship had plagued him for too long.

More from John White:

"When we came thither, we found the fort rased downe, but all the houses standing unhurt, saving that the neather roomes of them, and also of the forte, were overgrowen with Melons of divers sortes, and Deer within them, feeding on those Melons: so wee returned to our company, without hope of ever seeing any of the fifteene men living again."

Fate of Fifteen

In the morning after breakfast, Governor White and his assistants walked back to the pinnace. It was time to go around the north end to the west side of the island and check the fort for the 15 men. Manteo and the other settlers stayed behind while John White and his assistants sailed around the north end.

When the pinnace reached the fort, John searched the tree line and noticed he couldn't see a flag on the flag pole of the fort. He also couldn't see any of the wooden fort walls, only the earthworks. Upon reaching the shore, it was clear that the wooden walls of the fort had been burned but the nearby barracks were intact. The colonists spread out and walked around the fort murmuring to each other in little groups. Not finding the fifteen men was a major concern. The birds were chirping loudly high above the men's heads in the tall, skinny pines. Already the heat was to the point that their clothes were drenched with sweat.

"Governor White, come quick!" Chris Cooper shouted. Chris was on one knee looking at the ground. Beside him stood four others including Ananias Dare, John's son-in-law. They were all standing in a circle looking at the ground. John walked up to the silent group.

"What is it?" John asked as the men spread out to reveal a skeleton on the ground. The skull had a large hole in it and the sun had bleached the bones as white as snow. The skeleton had on a blue shirt that had been reduced to a torn up rag.

"Oh my God!" John said as he covered his mouth with one hand. The men looked at each other with fear in their eyes unsure what to say or do.

"We should bury him," Roger Prat said in a mono-tone voice. The men nodded yes and were about to start the process when a voice shouted for them.

"Over here! I have found a skeleton!" Roger Bailie was kneeling next to a skeleton just in front of the doorway to one of the buildings. Everyone began to feel uneasy. This time the skull had an arrow sticking out of the mouth. It was starting to become clear what had happened to Grenville's men. The men decided to bury the bones in two graves by the beach. A few prayers were said for the unknown skeletons and a long silence fell over the planters. Nothing could be heard but the wash of the gentle waves and the chirping of the birds. It was a very somber moment. They had only been on Roanoke Island for 14 hours and already they had the beginnings of a graveyard. The men walked back to the pinnace and discussed what they would tell the others at the settlement.

Meanwhile, the flyboat had reached Hatorask. The flyboat pulled up next to the *Lion*, which was at anchor with Fernando and a few men on board. The colonists inquired from the men on the *Lion* where the other planters were. Fernando actually told them the truth but was much grieved at their safe arrival. He never uttered a word of joy or relief in seeing them. The feeling was mutual.

The flyboat, like the *Lion,* had too deep of a draft to go into the sound so her colonists took longboats back and forth from the ship to Hatorask unloading all their supplies. Fernando's sailors helped in this process for about an hour then went back to fishing and crabbing at Hatorask. Once everything was unloaded, the colonists from the flyboat pressed on to Roanoke Island. The flyboat and her sailors remained off the coast, and eventually returned with the Lion to England after a week of rest and refitting of the ship.

The first of the flyboat's crew reached the beach at Roanoke just before the men in the pinnace returned from the fort. There they saw Manteo and some others spearing fish in a weir net Manteo had constructed. These men jumped and waved their arms when they saw the first longboat pull in. They waded into the sound with smiles and helped pull the boat to shore. Everyone was in a great mood to see each other and the additional supplies that they thought were lost. White and his assistants reached the settlement right after the men from the flyboat. They smiled and shook hands. When asked about the fort, they just said they didn't find anyone and that the walls of the fort had been burned. No one said anything about the bones. They didn't want to spoil the good mood. They also did not want the rest of the settlers to panic. Eventually they would have to tell the truth but now was not the moment.

The rest of the day was spent unloading supplies brought in by the flyboat. A well worn path wound its way from the settlement to the beach where the longboats landed with supplies. The settlers broke out their instruments and began to play and dance. John White and his assistants retired to the Governor's house with Manteo for a private conversation.

"Manteo we are sending you home to Croatoan with Captain Stafford and twenty others as soon as we can load the pinnace with enough supplies for a few days journey," White said slowly while he used hand gestures. Manteo nodded and smiled. Then White told him of the murders and the bones they found. Manteo's face became serious. He had a good idea who had done the killings, as did White. After all, Lane had given the mainland Indians plenty of reason to hate them.

White wanted Manteo to ask the Croatoan who had attacked the fifteen men and if any of them were still alive. He also wanted allies. If the mainland Indians had attacked, it was because they did not understand that these men were not Ralph Lane's brutes and White wanted to communicate through the Croatoan that they only wanted peace. He wanted to explain that they were not Lane's men.

Outside of the Governor's mansion, the rest of the settlers were making a home for themselves. They felled trees for additional houses, made shingles, and cleared land to plant crops. They figured the fifteen men they were looking for either went to Chesapeake to await the ships or else to Croatoan where they had a friendly relationship with the Indians and could also spot ships.

More from John White:

"same night at sunne-set went aland on the Island, in the place where our fifteene men were left, but we found none of them, nor any signe that they had bene there, saving onely wee found the bones of one of those fifteene, which the Savages had slaine long before."

'The 25 our Flyboate and the rest of our planters arrived all safe at Hatoraske, to the great joy and comfort of the whole company: but the Master of our Admirall Ferdinando grieved greatly at their safe coming: for hee purposely left them in the Bay of Portugal, and stole away from them in the night, hoping that the Master thereof, whose name was Edward Spicer, for that he never had bene in Virginia, would hardly finde the place,"

George Howe

Many of the colonists spent time catching crabs, clams, and fish from the sound. It was so easy to do and a wonderful change from the same meals they had had for so long on the ship. They set traps for rabbits and tried to hunt the deer that seemed to be everywhere.

One of the colonists, named George Howe, was by himself crabbing in knee deep of water. The mosquitoes were relentless. George smacked the back of his neck squashing one of them. He had filled a bucket half way with blue claw crabs and intended to go back to the settlement once it was full. The beauty of the land around him caused him to send up a prayer. George thanked the Lord for blessing him with the opportunity to come to such a fruitful land. George looked to the clouds as he silently prayed.

Without warning, an arrow sank into his gut then another into his hip. George fell into the water gripped with pain. He could feel his warm blood floating around his body. He swung his tiny hook in desperate rage but had not shaken the water from his eyes before two more arrows hit his chest and killed him.

George's body was found by Henry Pain, floating in the sound with 16 separate arrow wounds. His head was found in a near by bed of tall reeds. It had been smashed to pieces and his brains had stained the reeds purple. Henry clutched his mouth and started to gag when he saw his friend brutally murdered in this manner. He ran to a nearby group of three men that were shooting ducks and shouted to them.

At first they could not hear him because of the gunshots. He got their attention finally and shouted for them to follow him as he sprinted back to the body.

"Jesus! What sort of devils would do such a heinous act?" Henry Pain asked the other three men.

"By God what will we tell his son? He mustn't see the body. We should spare him the details," John Gibbs added. Roger Berry stood gripped with shock and just stared at the body, unable to speak.

Back at the settlement, George Howe's son was cutting timber when Henry Pain and John Gibbs approached him with the news. He immediately began to cry. Another graveyard was added next to the settlement and everyone gathered for the burial. After singing some hymns together, John White addressed the colonists.

"We are sending Manteo with Captain Stafford to Croatoan to learn of who committed this murder. We will renew our friendship with Manteo's people and see if they know where the other fifteen men are. In the meantime, those of us left on Roanoke are not to wander off alone. We will also post guards at night."

White searched the faces of the colonists as he spoke and saw his daughter Elinor. She was sweating and holding her round belly. Beside Elinor stood Mrs. Harvie quietly; she had an equally large stomach and a look of worry in her eyes.

Fernando was still sitting offshore of Hatorask giving his sailors time to improve their health and stock up on lumber. The live oaks of Hatorask were great for ship building. He decided to wait another two weeks before departing for England again. His sailors had a lot of fun shooting birds and roasting them on the beach to eat.

The following day, Captain Stafford left for Croatoan on the pinnace with Manteo and twenty men. The ride down was an easy one through the sound straight south. The tall pines of Croatoan lined the small hills that rose from the waters edge. The English could hear the steady beat of several drums as they approached shore. Manteo shouted in his native language to the woods ahead but got no reply.

When Stafford reached the beach at Croatoan, he was met by an army of men with bows and arrows. They looked as though they wanted to fight, until they heard Manteo's voice call to them. Upon hearing their own native tongue, they threw down their weapons. Stafford knew some of the Croatoan for he had lived there for a time at the end of Lane's botched settlement. He and his men anchored and waded through knee deep water to the beach on the soundside of Croatoan passing by many wier nets full of fish.

"Manteo how good to see you! We were worried you might never return!" Manteo's mother shouted as she emerged from the crowd of Indians on the beach. She embraced him. The two talked for several minutes while Stafford and his men stood around nervously. Manteo then turned to Stafford.

"They said they want to eat with us and will prepare a feast but they do not wish us to take any grain for there is only a little."

"Tell them we promise not to touch any of the grain and only wish to be friends again," Stafford said as he smiled at the crowd of Indians before him. Manteo relayed the message and followed his people into the woods to his native village. Slowly and tightly packed together, the English followed taking their guns and swords with them. The English clanked as they walked, for they were dressed in full armor. It was incredibly hot, even the water was in the upper 80's. The shade of the forest was a welcome change to the blistering sun beating down on the ship.

Stafford and his men were treated to a feast at Croatoan. They ate squash, cucumbers, and venison. After a good feast, Manteo sat with Stafford and interpreted the story of what happened to Grenville's men in great detail. The

Croatoan even knew that 13 of the 15 had survived the attack and fled to Hatorask. From there, they did not know where they went. Manteo then went on to say that it was the same tribe who killed George Howe that had killed Grenville's men.

"The warriors who killed Grenville's men were from Secotan, Aquscogoc, and Dasamonquepeu. The ones who killed George Howe live at Dasamonquepeu," Manteo said. Many of Manteo's people were talking to him all at once, wanting him to relate things to the English.

"They said a year ago, one of them was shot by Lane's men while he was off the island of Croatoan because he was mistaken for one of Wingina's men. He is lame now and will never walk again. They want a token or some sort of tattoo to show who they are so that this does not happen again."

Stafford nodded his head to Manteo and said they would be leaving for Roanoke in the morning. Captain Stafford was anxious to get to Dasamonquepeu and take revenge. The thought of George Howe's smashed brains enraged him. Then, Stafford caught site of the Croatoan man who had been shot by the English by mistake. He saw him sitting on a reed mat leaned against a felled tree, legs wasted away by atrophy and contracted into an awkward position. Cooler thoughts prevailed and Stafford asked Manteo a favor.

"Please ask if they will relay a message to Secotan, Aquscogoc, and Pomieok for me. Tell them we are not Lane's men. We have a new wiroans (leader) and wish to be friends. If they will accept us as friends, they can send word through the Croatoan or come to Roanoke with their answer themselves."

Manteo spoke with the Croatoan leaders and then told Stafford they agreed to try and that they should get a response within seven days. That night, Manteo spent a long deserved rest with his family and friends telling them all about England. Stafford and his men went and slept on the pinnace to get away from the ever present mosquitoes that seemed to prefer the tender and exotic white skin.

In the morning, it was time to return back to Roanoke. The night before some of Stafford's men had traded some trivial items such as cups and belts for fine raccoon hides and buckskins. They thanked the Croatoan and agreed upon a painted mark that would help the English to identify them as friends if they saw them off the island of Croatoan. It was simple: three parallel lines on the shoulder blade.

Meanwhile, back in the settlement John White and his assistants were gathered in the Governor's house. They were debating about who should go back to England with Fernando as that time was fast approaching. No one wanted to leave and get back on the ship with Fernando and his sailors. After a lot of noise, it was decided that Chris Cooper would go. However, the assistants debated again, and in the end they all signed a letter that they gave to John asking him to go. They felt he had the most influence back home and would be more likely to get supplies quickly.

Just as John White was exiting his meeting with the assistants, Stafford came running up to him.

"John we know who killed George Howe and the others. It was warriors from the mainland tribe, Wingina's old chiefdom. It does not surprise me much. After all, Lane killed many of them, cut their chief's head off, and burned a village not to mention the kidnapping of Skico. Still, perhaps they will understand that we had nothing to do with what Lane did."

Stafford spoke in a regretful tone and told John all he had learned from the Croatoan.

"Yes, but if we hear nothing in seven days, we must assume they are still our enemies. We should attack Dasamonquepeu in all haste for it is our biggest threat," John replied. He was under enough stress. He did not want to go back to England and leave his pregnant daughter but knew he must.

For the next seven days, a nor'easter storm raged so hard that the *Lion* had to weigh anchor and was forced out to sea in order to avoid being flung onto the beach. No word ever came to Roanoke from Secotan or the other Indian villages, so it was decided to attack Dasamonquepeu that night.

More excerpts from John White:

"The eight and twentieth, George Howe, one of our twelve Assistants was slaine by divers Savages,"

"These Savages being secretly hidden among high reedes, where oftentimes they find the Deere asleep, and so kill them, espied our man wading in the water alone, almost naked, without any weapon, save only a smal forked sticke, catching Crabs therewithal, and also being strayed two miles from his company, and shot at him in the water, where they gave him sixteen wounds with their arrowes: and after they had slaine him with their wooden swords, they beat his head in pieces, and fled over the water to the maine."

"On the thirtieth of July Master Stafford and twenty of our men passed by water to the Island of Croatoan, with Manteo, who had his mother, and many of his kinred dwelling in that island, of whom wee hoped to understand some newes of our fifteene men, but especially to learne the disposition of the people of the countrey towards us, and to renew our old friendship with them."

"We answered them, that neither their corne, nor any other nor any other thing of theirs should be diminished by any of us, and that our comming was onely to renew the old love, that was betweene us and them at the first, and to live with them as brethren and friends: which answere seemed to please them well, wherefore they requested us to walke up to their Towne, who there feasted us after their maner, and desired us earnestly, that there might bee some token or badge given them of us, whereby we might know them to be

our friends, when we met them any where out of the Towne or Island. They told us further, that for want of some such badge, divers of them were hurt the yeere before, being found out of the Island by Master Lane his company, where of they shewed us one, which at that very instant lay lame, and had lien of that hurt ever since: but they sayd, they knew our men mistooke them, and hurt them in stead of Winginos men, wherefore they held us excused. The next day we had conference further with them, concerning the people of Secotan, Aquascogoc, & Pomeiok, willing them of Croatoan to certifie the people of those townes, that if they would accept our friendship, we would willingly receive them againe, and that all unfriendly dealings past on both parts, should be utterly forgiven and forgotten. To this the chiefe men of Croatoan answered, that they would gladly doe the best they could, and within seven dayes, bring the Wiroances and chiefe Governours of those townes with them, to our Governour at Roanoak, or their answere."

A Baptism and a Baby

A t midnight, twenty-four men including Manteo and Captain Stafford departed from Roanoke for Dasamonquepeu. They took longboats and wrapped the oars in cloth once near the shore so that it would minimize the noise. They landed undetected and crept up on the village forming a line shaped like the letter 'C' with the concave end toward the village.

As Stafford crept through the trees that led to the village, he could smell smoke. Then he saw a fire burning with shadows passing in front of it. He jumped up with his pistol and fired the first shot. All at once, the line ripped a volley and the Indians scrambled for cover. As Stafford and his men reloaded, an Indian saw Stafford and came running to him.

"Stafford! Stafford!" The Indian knew his name.

Manteo then stood up and shouted, "they are Croatoan! Stop! Do not fire!" Indeed, they were Croatoan. They had come to raid the fields left by the people of Dasamonquepeu, who had abandoned the place after they killed George Howe. Chief Menatonan's wife was there as well with her baby strapped to her back. The Croatoan were not wearing the agreed upon tokens to show who they were and Manteo chastised them for being foolish. Luckily, only one man was wounded.

Stafford covered his face with his hand and was very apologetic. He asked that Menatonan's wife, baby, and the Croatoan accompany him back to Roanoke where they would care for the wounded and give them some English goods. The English helped the Croatoan finish clearing the fields around Dasamonquepeu before leaving for Roanoke. It was a huge harvest of pumpkins, grain, squash, and corn.

The Croatoan followed Stafford and his men to Roanoke in their canoes. Manteo elected to help row one of the canoes with some of his friends instead of ride with the English. As they landed on Roanoke, Stafford gathered everyone on the shore.

"I will go to the settlement ahead of everyone and tell them of our arrival to avoid another mishap. Please wait here." Captain Stafford looked right at Manteo as he spoke. Manteo relayed the message. There was one Croatoan man wounded in the shin. He sat in the sand with two others kneeling beside him. The shot had bounced off his shin bone but had broken it. He was in a lot of pain. The English had tied a cloth around the wound to stop the bleeding.

Stafford returned with two more men and a stretcher. They lifted the wounded man into the stretcher and started for the settlement. Everyone had baskets filled with food as they walked through the woods to the settlement.

When they reached the settlement all was forgiven and the settlers greeted them with open arms. The English men and women were all outside eager to see Manteo's people. They had a fire going and gifts ready to exchange with the Indians. Together, the Croatoan and the English feasted on the spoils of Dasamonquepeu and played music together. Music was the universal language. There was a lot of gawking by both parties and Manteo was busy translating for all.

Menatonan's wife was given a petticoat to take to her husband and a doll for her baby. She said nothing but took the gifts. It was only a year ago that Ralph Lane and his brutes had attacked her village and kidnapped her oldest son Skico. As for this new group of English, they seemed dangerous despite the kindness they were showing now. Why hours ago they had attacked their own allies by mistake. They seemed a little trigger happy. It was very late at night now yet no one slept aside from Menatonan's baby.

In the morning, when the colonists emerged from their houses, the Croatoan were gone. They left a pile of animal skins, uppowoc, and pearls by the fire pit. Manteo was missing but came walking into the settlement with two dead rabbits and a smile.

"Well, you're up early. I thought you might have gone home with your kindred," John White said as he walked up to Manteo. John was in good spirits after the friendly feast. It was extremely windy and John's hat flew off. Dyonis Harvie picked it up and handed it back to John.

"My Margeny is very near to giving birth, as is your daughter Elinor. We should have the babies baptized by Sir Stevens." John was suddenly hit with an epiphany. He was watching Manteo skin the rabbits and thought Manteo should also be baptized.

The following Sunday, Manteo was baptized and given the title Lord of Roanoke and Dasamonquepeu by the planters. Manteo had been helping the colonists to build weir nets, to catch fish, and had shown them where to get fresh water. The Croatoan much frequented Roanoke to trade goods and all were happy. The ceremony was simple with all 116 (Howe was dead) English present and three Croatoan. Manteo was dunked in the sound by Sir Stevens then given a bible. Manteo could not read the bible. In fact, most of the planters couldn't read it either for it was written in Latin. Manteo loved his new friends and wished to take them to Croatoan where they could live together and learn from each other, but still the winds howled relentlessly.

It was time for the *Lion* and the flyboat to return to England with Governor White but they could not depart until the seas calmed down. For Governor White, this was a blessing, because he wanted more time with his daughter. He felt as though the storm was created by God so that he could be present for the birth of his granddaughter.

On August 18th, Elinor Dare went into labor. It was just about noon when her water broke. Jane Pierce was with

Elinor in her cabin when it happened. They had just sat down to eat some fruit when both realized water was running from Elinor's chair to the ground. Jane called out to Ananias who was just outside.

"The baby is coming! Hurry!" Ananias was filled with a near panic as he raced inside. Elinor was sweating and groaning with pain. Jane had done some midwifery back in England and things were not so different here. Jane kept Ananias busy by putting him to use. She had him gather some fresh water, collect towels, and twine for the tying of the cord.

The entire settlement had gathered around the outside of the house while Ananias, Jane, and Elinor remained inside. The people outside could hear the pain Elinor was going through. John stood holding his hat in both hands praying for the safety of his daughter and the baby. Margeny Harvie, who was very close to birth herself, looked a bit nervous by the noises she was hearing.

Inside the house, Ananias held Elinor's hand while she pushed the baby out and squeezed Ananias's fingers to the point they were purple. Jane was at the foot of the bed, encouraging Elinor and doing the best she could do deliver the baby.

Finally, John could hear a baby crying. Everyone outside cheered and waited for someone to come outside. Eventually, Ananias emerged from the house looking quite pale and addressed the crowd with a weak smile.

"It's a beautiful baby girl! We have named her Virginia after this virgin land." John welled up with tears of joy and gave Ananias a great hug.

"Is Elinor doing well?"

"See for yourself. She is fine." John and Ananias walked inside together to see Elinor resting and holding Virginia Dare, who was wrapped in a green cloth and already nursing. Jane was sitting next to them admiring the baby.

It wasn't long after the birth that the flyboat and the *Lion* were ready, having ridden out the nor'easter and loaded the ships with letters and gifts from the colonists to their loved ones back home. Fernando was eager to get back before the tempest (Hurricane) season.

Before leaving, John had a meeting with his son-in-law and the other eleven assistants. He knew that Roanoke Island was not the best place for a settlement, considering it's proximity to a nation that hated them and a lack of fresh water.

"I shall return again at once. If for some reason you leave the island of Roanoke, write the name of the place you are going to on a tree. If you leave for reasons of danger mark the tree with a cross underneath it." With these parting words, John White left for England, but only after kissing Virginia Dare on her sweet head.

He watched his daughter and granddaughter disappear as he departed for the ships off Hatorask. Elinor was sitting by the shore on a reed mat holding Virginia in one hand and waving with the other. It would be the last time John White ever saw them.

Captain Stafford also returned to England on the flyboat. The colonists were left with twenty longboats, more than enough to transport the lot of them from the island to the mainland or to another island. When last seen, the colony was trading with the Croatoan and at war with the mainland Indians. Manteo was still with them and a great help.

More from John White:

"The eight of August, the Governour having long expected the comming of the Wiroanses of Pomeiok, Aquascogoc, Secota, and Dasamonguepeuk, seeing that the seven dayes were past, within which they promised to come in, or to send their answeres by the men of Croatoan, and no tidings of them heard, being certainly also informed by those men of Croatoan, that the remnant of Wingina his men,

which were left alive, who dwelt at Dasamonquepeuk, were they which had slaine George Howe, and were also at the driving of our eleven Englishmen from Roanoak, hee thought to deferre revenge thereof no longer. Wherefore the same night about midnight, he passed over the water, accompanied with Captaine Stafford, and 24 men, wherof Manteo was one, whom we tooke with us to be our guide to the place where those Savages dwelt, where he behaved himselfe toward us as a most faithfull Englishman."

"but we were deceived, for those Savages were our friends, and were come from Croatoan to gather the corne & fruit of that place, because they understood our enemies were fled immediately after they had slaine George Howe, and for haste had left all their corne, Tobacco, and Pompions standing in such sort, that al had bene devoured by the birds, and Deere, if it had not bene gathered in time: but they had like to have payd deerely for it: for it was so darke, that they being naked, and their men and women appareled all so like others, wee knew not but that they were al men: and if that one of them which was a Wiroances wife had not had a child at her backe, shee had bene slaine in stead of a man, and as hap was, another Savage knew master Stafford, and ran to him, calling him by his name, whereby hee was saved. Finding our selves thus disappointed of our purpose, we gathered al the corne, Pease, Pompions, and Tabacco that we found ripe, leaving the rest unspoiled, and tooke Menatoan his wife, with the yong child, and the other Savages with us over the water to Roanoak. Although the mistaking of these Savages somewhat grieved Manteo, yet he imputed their harme to their owne folly, saying to them, that if their Wiroances had kept their promise in comming to the Governour at the day appointed, they had not knowen that mischance.

The 13 of August our Savage Manteo, by the commandement of Sir Walter Ralegh, was christened in

Roanoak, and called Lord thereof, and as Dasamonguepek, in reward of his faithfull service.

The 18 Elenor, daughter of the Governour, and wife to Ananias Dare one of the Assistants, was delivered of a daughter in Roanoak, and the same was christened there the Sonday following, and because this child was the first Christian borne in Virginia, shee was named Virginia. By this time our ships had unladen the goods and victuals of the planters, and began to take in wood, and fresh water, and to new calke and trimme them for England: the planters also prepared their letters and tokens to send backe into England."

"The Governour being at the last through their extreame intreating constrayned to returne into England, having then but halfe a dayes respite to prepare himselfe for the same, departed from Roanoak the seven and twentieth of August in the morning,"

The Abandoned Colony

It would be three years before John White could return to Roanoke. In his first attempt in 1588, the English attacked a French ship and were defeated. John White himself was wounded but did make it back to England. At this point the war with Spain was heating up to a climax, and Queen Elizabeth would not spare any more of her ships or Captains. In 1588, the Spanish Armada attacked England and was defeated due in a large part to a great storm, which of course the English credited God for sending.

Finally in 1590, John White, Captain Spicer, and Captain Stafford were able to return to Roanoke. On the way there, they saw columns of smoke rising from Kindrick's Mount (Salvo on Hatteras Island), but they did not stop there. They continued north and anchored off Hatorask then took longboats across the inlet to Roanoke. This was not an easy process. While crossing the inlet, John White was in a longboat with nine others and Captain Spicer was in another longboat with ten others. The waves were fairly big with a northeast wind behind them. Captain Spicer's longboat was crushed by a wave half way through the inlet and rolled completely over three times. The constant barrage of white water from the waves that followed made it impossible to stand or swim.

John watched in horror as Spicer and his men clung to the longboat that was being pushed around upside down and washed over by huge walls of rushing white water. They could hear the desperate men yelling for help. Immediately, John White's boat came to their aide. The best swimmers of John White's boat tore off their shoes and shirts and jumped in to save those that were still treading water from Spicer's boat. They pulled four of the eleven men from the water and got them safely back to White's boat. However, Captain Spicer and six others did not make it and were never seen again. White's longboat returned to the ships to unload the half drowned men and regroup with supplies since all of the supplies in Spicer's boat were lost to the sea.

Back on the ships, the deaths of Spicer and the others so disturbed the sailors that they argued not to look for the planters any further. White was irate and pointed out the plight of the planters and his daughter and granddaughter. After a lot of bad noise, it was decided to make another attempt to cross the inlet. This time 19 men in two longboats made it safely through the inlet to the sound where the waters were comparatively calm.

They arrived off the coast of Roanoke just after sunset. It was cloudy out, blocking the stars and moon. It was so dark that they sailed past the settlement site by a quarter mile. Then suddenly they saw a light. It was a great fire that they could see through the woods. They anchored opposite the fire and sounded trumpets and sang English songs but got no reply. The fire slowly got smaller then disappeared. It was too dark to try and navigate through the virgin forest so the men slept in the longboats. The mosquitoes were vicious. The warm night air was filled with the sounds of bull frogs, crickets, and the occasional call of an owl.

At daybreak, the English landed on the island and raced to the spot of the fire. All they found were some burnt out stumps still smoldering. Sometimes the Roanoke Indians had used fire to signal to passing ships that they wished to trade. White then led his crew to the west side of the island to the beach. From there, the men rounded the northern point of the island to the cliffs on the northeast side of the island and made their way up the sandy bank to the woods. It was here that they saw a clue to the colony's whereabouts. A tree had the letters CRO carved on it. The men stopped and looked at the tree.

"Cro...that must mean Croatoan. It makes sense. Manteo being from there and his people our friends and allies. I told them to carve a cross if they left for reasons of danger," John said to his friend Captain Cooke. Cooke and the others agreed that it made sense for the planters to go to Croatoan. John and the others searched the tree and a few other trees nearby but saw no cross. This was a great relief to John and not the least bit surprising. Still he wanted to press on to the settlement.

When the men reached the spot of the settlement, they found a palisade had been built in a large circle around where the houses once stood. All of the buildings had been taken down. This was not as strange as it sounds. The construction used in building these houses was one that held wooden beams together by wooden joints. The houses were like puzzles, easily taken down and moved. Between the wooden beams was a clay/sand mixture much like stucco. This could be made again with little labor. It is very likely that the colonists took apart and moved these dwellings to their new settlement.

John White had already seen a tree with the letters CRO carved on it. Now, on a large tree that made up part of the palisade was the full word CROATOAN. Once again, the word was written in all capital letters and the tree had had the bark removed on the side that had Croatoan carved on it. Now John was sure of what he had already supposed CRO had meant to indicate. Again, no cross or sign of distress was found.

"We were right! They did move to Croatoan. Perhaps they saw our ships go by and that is why we saw smoke rising from Kindrick's Mount as we passed on our way here. Maybe some of them returned in their small boats to meet us. Let us go now to the creek where the boats were kept." John had little concern in his voice and planned to go to Croatoan immediately once back on the ships. He and his company found none of the small cannon left to the colony inside of the palisade but did find some iron bars and four fowling guns overgrown with grass. Once at the point of a creek where the boats had been kept, White and his men saw none of the boats or pinnaces that had been left with the planters.

It was very clear that Roanoke Island had been completely abandoned by the colonists. The houses were gone, the boats were gone and as agreed upon before White left in 1587, there was a tree spelling out in capital letters where the colony had gone to.

Sadly, White never made it to Croatoan to relieve the colony. Instead, the waves picked up and the ships lost three out of four anchors as well as some fresh water casks. Seven had already drowned and spirits were low. The ships were almost driven into the shore when passing the point at Kindrick's Mountains (Rodanthe to Salvo). It was here that most of the anchor cables broke. Today, the area is know as Wimble Shoals and is second only to Diamond Shoals in quantity of shipwrecks on the entire East Coast. The ships simply gave up and went back to England without ever going to Croatoan. The original plan was to go to St. Johns or Trinidad and then return laden with supplies to Croatoan on the return voyage to England. For on the way home, they would follow the Gulf Stream north again to Croatoan which even John White agreed to do. It did not work out due to a northwest storm that blew them far out to sea. No other attempt to reach Croatoan was made for twelve years and it was not much of an attempt for it never reached Croatoan either. Thus, the colony was abandoned at Croatoan.

Excerpts from John White:

"Captaine Spicer came to the entrance of the breach with his mast standing up, and was halfe passed over, but by the rash and undiscreet styrage of Ralph Skinner his Masters mate, a very dangerous Sea brake into their boate and overset them quite, the men kept the boat some in it, and some hanging on it, but the next sea set the boat on ground, where it beat so, that some of them were forced to let goe their hold, hoping to wade ashore; but the Sea still beat them

downe, so that they could neither stand nor swimme, and the boat twise or thrise was turned the keele upward, whereon Captaine Spicer and Skinner hung untill they sunke, & were seene no more. But foure that could swimme a litle kept themselves in deeper water and were saved by Captain Cookes meanes, who so soone as he saw their oversetting, stripped himselfe, and four other that could swimme very well, & with all haste possible rowed unto them, & saved foure. They were a 11 in all, & 7 of the chiefest were drowned,"

"In all this way we saw in the sand the print of the Salvages feet of 2 or 3 sorts troaden ye night, and as we entred up the sandy banke upon a tree, in the very browe thereof were curiously carved these fair Romane letters C R O: which letters presently we knew to signifie the place, where I should find the planters seated, according to a secret token agreed upon betweene them & me at my last departure from them, which was, that in any wayes they should not faile to write or carve on the trees or posts of the dores the name of the place where they should be seated;"

'I willed them, that if they should happen to be distressed in any of those places, that then they should carve over the letters or name, a Crosse in this forme, but we found no such signe of distresse. And having well considered of this, we passed toward the place where they were left in sundry houses, but we found the houses taken downe, and the place very strongly enclosed with a high palisado of great trees, with cortynes and flankers very Fort-like, and one of the chiefe trees or postes at the right side of the entrance had the barke taken off, and 5 foote from the ground in fayre Capitall letters was graven CROATOAN without any crosse or signe of distresse; this done, we entred into the palisado, where we found many barres of Iron, two pigges of Lead, foure yron fowlers, Iron sacker- shotte, and such like heavie things, throwen here and there, almost overgrowen with

grasse and weedes. From thence wee went along by the water side, towards the point of the Creeke to see if we could find any of their botes or Pinnisse, but we could perceive no signe of them, nor any of the last Falkons and small Ordinance which were left with them, at my departure from them."

"*I greatly joyed that I had safely found a certaine token of their safe being at Croatoan, which is the place where Manteo was borne, and the Savages of the Iland our friends.*"

"*The next Morning it was agreed by the Captaine and my selfe, with the Master and others, to wey anchor, and goe for the place at Croatoan, where our planters were: for that then the winde was good for that place,*"

"*On the 28 the winde changed, and it was sette on foule weather every way: but this storme brought the winde West and Northwest, and blewe so forcibly, that wee were able to beare no sayle, but our fore- course halfe mast high, wherewith wee ranne upon the winde perforce, the due course for England,*"

Later Attempts

In 1602, Sir Walter Raleigh sent an expedition to look for the colony but they never went to Croatoan. Instead, they went to Cape Fear, traded with the Coree Indians, and returned to England. In 1603, King James took the throne. He hated Raleigh and immediately put him in jail for treason, then had his head cut off. King James made no attempt to go to Croatoan to get the colony. In fact, he ran all of the proprietors of the voyage out of the country or underground. Even Thomas Harriot was driven into hiding. None of Sir Walter Raleigh's friends were liked by King James. James was Catholic and had no problems with Spain. After all, the Outer Banks had been selected by the former ruler, Queen Elizabeth, as an ideal place to raid Spanish ships that took the Gulf Stream back to Europe. Raliegh's half brother Humphrey Gilbert, had been issued a patent by Queen Elizabeth that gave him the rights to all the riches of the New World. When Gilbert drowned off of Newfoundland the patent passed to Raleigh. King James could not kill this patent by simply killing Raleigh for it would pass to his heirs. The only way to kill the patent was to not contact the colony ever again. Perhaps this is why no one ever went to look for the colony at Croatoan or for that matter at all once James took the throne.

In 1607, another English colony went to the New World. They landed in modern day Virginia and founded Jamestown, named after King James. It had been twenty years since John White had waved good-bye to his daughter and granddaughter on the shore of Roanoke Island. Clear indication had been made by the planters that they had gone to Croatoan and yet no one ever went there. Even after Jamestown was settled, no one ever went down to Croatoan. Instead, they asked the Indians around Jamestown about the colonists and were told four of the colonists were alive in a town called Panauuaiooc. This town is present day Chocowinity and the Indians that lived there migrated from Croatoan according to their descendants as well as genealogical records. Did anyone from Jamestown check it out? NO! It is likely that being twenty years later, the colonists at this point had split up, had children, and so on.

The next mention of the colonists comes from the Coree Indians at Cape Fear. These Indians told the Cape Fear English colony in 1669 that "your kindred of Roanoke have been adopted and assimilated into the Hatteras tribe." Was anything done? Nope.

So when did someone finally go to Croatoan and what did they find? Finally, in 1701 John Lawson goes to Hatteras Island/Croatoan. The Croatoan Indians have an oral history that says the colony of 1587 came to Croatoan and stayed there. They reported this oral history to Lawson in 1701. John Lawson was the first known European to go to Croatoan since the 16th century voyages that has surviving records. He recorded his findings in a book titled, 'A New Voyage to Carolina,' which can still be purchased today.

Lawson noted in his writings some of the Indians at Croatoan had grey/blue eyes and that many of these Indians wore English clothes. Lawson also wrote that the Croatoan/ Hatteras Indians reported a ship that they called Raleigh's ship would sometimes still appear there.

Here are a few quotes from John Lawson's 'A New Voyage to Carolina':

"Hatteras Indians these are them that wear English dress."

"A farther Confirmation of this we have from the Hatteras Indians, who either then lived on Ronoak-Island, or much frequented it. These tell us, that several of their Ancestors were white People, and could talk in a Book, as we do; the Truth of which is confirm'd by gray Eyes being found frequently amongst these Indians, and no others. They value themselves extremely for their Affinity to the English, and are ready to do them all friendly Offices."

"I cannot forbear inserting here, a pleasant Story that passes for an uncontested Truth amongst the Inhabitants of this Place; which is, that the Ship which brought the first Colonies, does often appear amongst them, under Sail, in a gallant Posture, which they call Sir Walter Raleigh's Ship; And the truth of this has been affirm'd to me, by Men of the best Credit in the Country."

The rest of this book will focus on the modern day search for the colonists and dispel some of the ludicrous theories about the lost/abandoned colony of 1587. A lot of myths and lies are out there about the colony that need to be addressed as well as the facts. I will also trace the migration of the Croatoan Indians from Hatteras Island to the mainland and their connection to the Lumbee Indians of today.

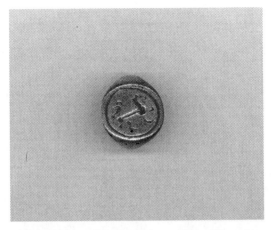

Gold signet ring from the Croatoan site. The ring may have belonged to "Master" Kendall, a member of the 1585-86 expedition.

Late 16th century snaphaunce gunlock from the Croatoan site.

Photos of the ring and gunlock from Croatoan used by permission of Dr. David Phelps, Director of the Croatoan Archaeological Project.

Pottery sherd found by Scott Dawson in 2006. Clay pots were mostly used to cook vegetables and meats. The mineral rich left over water was then consumed or used to water crops. Clay pots were also used to heat up tree sap into resin to use in the construction of canoes and houses. Tiny chunks of shell were added to the clay to make it stronger.

Pottery found by Scott Dawson and Joey Crum. This is what they look like before being cleaned.

1759 Croatoan land deed giving land to the Hatteras Indians. Coastland Times photo.

Inside the bottom of a cord wrapped Croatoan pot. The large piece was found by Scott Dawson and the smaller by Scott Meekins. Both found in Buxton 2008, at the same location but 6 months apart! This pot had a cone shaped bottom.

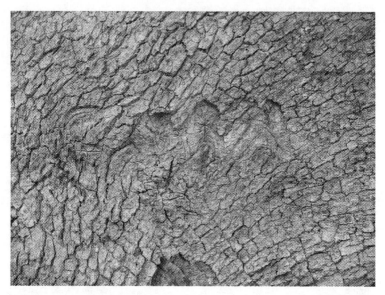

Close-up of the Cora tree on modern day Hatteras Island. Photo taken by Scott Dawson

Finding Croatoan

There exists a myth that some seem to believe that the location of Croatoan is a mystery. This lie has even wiggled its way into some North Carolina textbooks. Croatoan is mentioned in the primary sources countless times and appears clearly labeled on John White's maps. In John White's 1593 letter to Richard Hakluyt, he wrote "…I was deeply joyful for the certain token of their safe arrival at Croatoan, where the savages of the island were our friends, and where Manteo was born." Even the latitude of the Northeast corner of Croatoan was given in White's letter.

Anyone who has read the primary sources or looked at John White's maps or De Bry's engravings knows where Croatoan was/is. It is the lower half of modern-day Hatteras Island, namely Buxton, Frisco, and Hatteras villages. It has also been positively identified by archeologists such as Dr. David Phelps, not to mention the families that still live there now who can trace their family history back to the Croatoan Indians.

Phillip Amadas and Arthur Barlow landed on Croatoan in 1584 and described the island as about 20 miles long running from east to west and about six miles wide. Today, it is no different from east to west but due to erosion the island is only about 3 miles wide at the widest point. John Lawson gives the latitude of an inlet near Diamond Shoals as 35'20". Today, that latitude would be just north of Buxton at a place called Canadian Hole by the locals, which is exactly what it looks like on John White's map. In addition, in 1962, an inlet formed in this exact same spot due to the Ash Wednesday

Storm, which was 5-6 days of a terrible nor'easter. The inlet persisted for months. The locals tried throwing in their old junk cars to close up the inlet and with some success, but eventually the state had to fill it in and close the inlet.

Some people who are not from the area get confused when they look at White's map because they see two prominent capes instead of one like you have now on the Outer Banks. Well, right where Rodanthe is today there once was a large cape. You can still see tree stumps along the ocean floor as well as on the beach there and all of the natives will tell you how the cape rapidly eroded upon the dredging of Oregon Inlet.

The next step is to look at when the earliest European settlers lived on Hatteras, besides the Lost Colony. Here we have a huge problem. Most of the earliest settlers for Hatteras were shipwreck victims or squatters from Jamestown. Neither of these groups kept any surviving records.

Cape Hatteras is so isolated that no records of the earliest settlers there were ever recorded. Hatteras Island has been a part of Albemarle County, Currituck County, Hyde County, and now Dare County. So far, the nearest any courthouse has been to Croatoan is the one currently in Manteo, 72 miles away. Not until 1957 would there be a paved road the length of Hatteras Island, and not until 1964 was there a bridge from the island to the mainland. It was the 1960's, before there were police or a doctor on the island. Due to the extreme isolation of the island, most of the paper trails do not start until there is a courthouse. This creates a problem for researchers. However, there are a few surviving paper trails leading you to births, deaths, and marriages written in family bibles, letters, and journals that predate the courthouse, not to mention gravestones.

When Albemarle County officially started in 1650, it was full of 'illegals' from Jamestown, Virginia. It is estimated that over 2,000 Europeans lived in Albemarle County before any deeds were recorded. They simply purchased land from the Indians directly and never told anyone. In addition to this, goods came and went tax free, which eventually lead to Culpepper's rebellion. Thomas Miller was put in charge of checking ships at the inlets. The British Crown wanted to tax all cargos going in and out of the colonies. Miller recorded the names of all those who avoided the taxes and was given the position of Governor in 1677. In the colonial records that cover this rebellion, many Lost Colony surnames pop up on Hatteras Island. Due to these colonial records, we know for certain that some English settlers with livestock and with Lost Colony surnames occupied Hatteras Island by 1664.

In 1711, the Hatteras Indians fought on the English side of the Tuscarora War and were given 16 bushels of corn from the public store by the colonial government. Then in 1733, we have Moseley's very detailed map of North Carolina, which shows Croatoan with an Indian village located on the soundside of Buxton, and two English villages. The English villages are labeled "Gibb" and "Neal." More than likely these towns were run by the Gibbs and O'Neal families, both of which can be traced to the start of the paper trail for Hatteras Island families. Gibbs is also the surname of one of the Lost Colonists.

Then, in 1759 Arthur Dobbs, the colonial governor of North Carolina, issues a 200 acre land grant to the Hatteras Indians who sport many of the colony's surnames such as Gibbs, Berry, and Payne to name a few. If this isn't enough evidence for the colony going to Croatoan keep in mind that Croatoan is exactly where all of the 16th century English artifacts have been found as well as European skeletons found in a mass grave. This information has been published recently in Down East magazine, Our State, and National Geographic. DNA testing was done on descendants of the Payne family with relatives of Henry Payne back in England and a positive match was found. This story was presented on the History Channel.

Questions and Theories, Facts and Myths

The natural question to ask is: why didn't anyone ever go to Croatoan to look for the colony? It is easy to blame King James. In 1603, when Queen Elizabeth died and King James took over, the fate of the colony was sealed. As stated before, King James hated Sir Walter Raleigh and could not have cared less about Raleigh's colony. In fact, King James sent Raleigh on many near-suicide missions and then eventually locked him in the Tower of London for twelve years before he had Raleigh's head cut off for treason.

We will never know for sure why no one went back to Croatoan, but what we do know is that no real effort was ever made to go to Croatoan to find the colony. *Abandoned Colony* is a more appropriate term for these settlers rather than *Lost Colony*, for they spelled out in capital letters where they were going (Croatoan, a place the English had been to and even lived several times before), yet **no one ever went there to look for them**.

This colony was abandoned, not lost. The colonists wrote down where they were going and no one ever looked there! Everyone knew where Croatoan was back then just as we know now. That has never been a mystery, unless you get all of your information from the famous outdoor drama, which is about the equivalent of Disney's <u>Pocahontas</u> in accuracy.

So what happened after they reached Croatoan? One theory has the colonists migrating from Croatoan to the mainland. When one considers that Wingina's old tribe still hated the English and had in fact killed George Howe, it makes sense that the colony would seek help from a tribe not on the mainland such as the Croatoan who were still their allies, hence the carving of Croatoan on the tree.

Interestingly, back in 1584, Barlowe had been told that the people just to the South of Secotan were bitter enemy's of Wingina. These people are collectively called the Nuesiok but are really several tribes all in league with each other. The tribe closest to the Croatoan was the Coree. They lived principally in two towns called Coranine and Cwarennoc. In the heart of one of the Indian villages on Croatoan (Frisco), is a tree with the word CORA carved or burned into it. This tree is estimated to be at least a thousand years old and is a massive water oak (17 feet in circumference). The word CORA is written in all capital letters just as the CROATOAN carving in Roanoke, and no one knows how the word CORA got there. There is a legend that this tree was a hanging tree and that a witch named Cora was hung there, but during the hanging lightening struck the tree and she turned into a panther and ran off. Obviously, that never happened, but the legend has been told for hundreds of years giving us some idea as to how old the carving is. Did the colonists write the word CORA on the tree to indicate they were migrating to the Coree villages?

Less than a mile from the CORA tree, a major discovery was made in the 1950's. While digging to put in canals for the island's first organized subdivision, a drag-line operator named Martin "Flay" Kemp found some wooden caskets made out of juniper. They were accidentally dug up during the dragging process. No one had ever heard of a graveyard being there or the canals would have been dug somewhere else. These caskets were wider at the shoulder end and became narrower as they reached the feet. They were dug out canoes that had been fashioned together with wooden pegs. Sadly, these caskets were literally smashed and thrown away, and all archaeological information that could have been extracted from them is forever gone. Later,

Martin Kemp told the story of disposing of these caskets because he felt so guilty about having discarded them, rather than reburying them. His daughter still lives and works in Dare County today, and carries on her father's oral history of this major archaeological find. In addition, a book titled 'The Five Lost Colonies of Dare,' written by Mary Wood Long, discusses this find of Juniper caskets by Mr.Kemp.

In the 1990s, and again in 2006, archaeological digs were conducted at what has been confirmed to be the Croatoan Village site in modern day Buxton. Interestingly, the pottery found during the Croatoan digs is very unique. It is reheated grog pottery. In fact, the only other place this type of pottery has been found is where Coranine once stood. It is white in color instead of the usual brown or black. It is a pot or bowl that is cooked once and then smashed to pieces and mixed with more clay and shells, and then reheated. Evidently this makes the pottery stronger. The pots were actually put on a fire pit upside down so that the inside of the pots were blackened by the fire and the outside was usually a tan/grey color. If a good bit of the pottery at Croatoan came from Coranine (estimated at 11%) then they must have traded with each other or possibly were a part of the same tribe. After all, Coranine is directly across the sound from Croatoan. In addition, there is no clay with which to make pottery on Hatteras Island so the clay had to come from the mainland.

So, did the Lost Colony migrate over to the mainland in the area of the Coree Indians, or the Coranine village? Remember, the Jamestown area Indians reported that some of the colonists were at what is now Chocowinity. Well Cwarennoc, the other principal town of the Coree *is* Chocowinity. Hence, more evidence to support the theory of the colonists going to CORA. Did they leave us another message on this ancient Croatoan tree?

Another theory has the colonists assimilating into the Lumbee tribe. The Lumbee tell us some of their ancestors migrated inland from Croatoan in 1696 after an epidemic of disease struck the coast.

In the 1880's the Lumbee Indians who are the assimilation of several tribes including the Croatoan, pensioned Congress for recognition. In 1913, the Lumbee and the Federal courts had a long case that the Lumbee won. They wanted schools and the same rights as had been given to the Cherokee and other NC tribes. So far, they had not been recognized as a tribe because most were Christians, spoke English, and appeared to be a mixed race people. The Federal government was shown enough evidence to yield to the Lumbee demands and the entire case is in the Library of Congress if anyone wants to read about it. These people still maintain that they are descendents of the Lost Colony of 1587 and once again genealogy seems to back this statement up. Around 50 of the Lost Colony surnames are found in the Lumbee tribe/nation.

However, in 1701 there were still 80 Croatoan Indians living on Hatteras Island wearing English clothes and some with grey eyes according to Lawson, so some of the Croatoan must have elected not to migrate.

There are many theories as to what happened to the Lost Colony, but they all start with the colony going to Croatoan or at least a portion of them.

Genealogical Evidence and Migration

The Lost Colony Center for Science and Research spent time researching the oldest deeds they could find for the land they were digging on in Croatoan. From these deeds, they found several last names that are still common on the island today, such as Elks, Farrow, Berry, Jennette, and Gibbs. In the public records, these families were referred to as Hatteras Indians, which is synonymous with Croatoan Indians. Mr. Willard with help from dozens of volunteers, traced many of these names back to the earliest recorded deeds in the county. As stated before, in the earliest part of European settlement in North Carolina, no one bothered to get a deed recorded because there wasn't a courthouse to record one in. Most Europeans living on the Outer Banks in those days were squatters or shipwreck survivors.

The paper trails are a bit of a dead end but they get us close enough that perhaps DNA testing can help. Once again, the problem is funding. For now, archaeology can help prove what is already obvious from the primary sources, that the colony moved to Croatoan. What is not clear is how they faired after getting there.

Now the research becomes really interesting. Remember the unique pottery only found in Croatoan and the Coree village on the mainland? That is where the genealogy takes us. In conjunction with the genealogy, the maps after 1680 start to place the word Croatoan not just on the southern half of Hatteras Island but on the mainland too, in the area of Mann's Harbor.

The oral history of East Lake, NC states that there were Indians with guns that lived in their area of the mainland in the 1700's. A timber company under John Grey Blount, went into the East Lake area in the early 1700's and they were chased out by Indians who spoke a sort of broken English and said they had lived there for over 100 years. These Indians also lived in European styled houses that were still visible in the 1840's. These people raised and ate cattle and practically died off from a black tongue disease. Barbra Midgette, of Buxton, found out the black tongue disease was anthrax from a 7,000 word 17th century dictionary. A disease people usually get from horses or cattle.

A paper company from West Virginia in the 1950's made an interesting discovery that may shed some light on just who those Indians were. Martin "Flay" Kemp was again operating a drag line in this area and found caskets made of hollowed out juniper logs that were held together by wooden pegs and grave stones in the heavily wooded area called Beechland, right next to East Lake. The caskets came out of a large mound and were reburied in a different area by the men who found them. Wait didn't this same strange occurrence happen in Frisco on Hatteras Island? Sure did.

Once again, no one in the area was aware of a grave-yard at this location. This area is just west of Roanoke Island and is labeled Croatoan on all the maps made in the late 1600's. If the colony was assimilated into the Croatoan tribe, then they could live on any land the Croatoan or their allies held. Did they migrate across the sound at some point and start living in Beechland or near enough to bury their dead there? Did some migrate to the mainland while some stayed on Hatteras Island?

We all know about Jamestown founded in 1607. We all know about the maps John White made in 1585. Notice the difference in the names of the Indian villages on John White's maps verses the earliest maps that came out of Jamestown. All of the villages in Wingina's old territory change names. Where Dasamonquepeu once stood is the word Croatoan. In addition, Croatoan is also still found in its original spot where modern day Buxton is today. Did the Croatoan and Corees help the English conquer their enemies at Dasamonquepeu? What about Pomieok, Secotan, and Aquscogoc? They are all replaced with new names. One of which is Coranine, which comes from the Coree Indians. This had to happen sometime between 1587 and 1607. The names of the villages of the chiefdom that had been killing the English are replaced by Croatoan and Coree names...

The oldest recorded marriage license for Hatteras Island is of Thomas Hooper and Johana Kinkett in 1689. Miss Kinkett was the daughter of Chief Kinnakeet, the old name of the town of Avon, three miles north of Croatoan. On John White's 1585 map, this town is called Paquiwoc. When did Paquiwoc become Kinnakeet? Probably the same time Pomieok, Secotan, and the others changed names. Regardless of why, the point is the names all change. Mattamuskeet Lake replaced what had been called Paquuyp. It seems like some war was going on in the New World between 1587 and 1607. After all, just before John White left the colony in 1587, the colonists and the Croatoan had been responsible for the raiding of Dasamonquepeu and all of her fields. The English were still angry about the murder of George Howe and the Croatoan initiated the raiding of Roanoke village on the mainland. All throughout 1585 and into 1586, the Croatoan continued to feed the English, almost half of whom lived on Croatoan under Edward Stafford. They did this despite Wingina's eventual refusal to do so. Manteo was even with Lane when the English killed the chief and Manteo was trusted with a gun.

More evidence for friction between the coastal tribes and the Mainland can be found in 1711. 1711 is the famous Tuscarora War where the coastal Indians and the Europeans in the area were attacked by the Tuscarora. The town of Bath was burned to the ground and over 300 settlers were killed. The few Croatoan who were still on Hatteras Island were virtually annihilated. Troops from South Carolina had to be brought in to squash the rebellion.

An interesting side note, the oldest <u>recorded</u> deed of the Croatoan site was to a man named John Elks. This man was married to a descendent of Mary Ormond of Bath. This is the same woman who was also married to Blackbeard and was his final of 14 wives. Much of Blackbeard's crew came from the Outer Banks. Thomas Miller, the quartermaster of Blackbeard's ship was from Kinnakeet and is found on tax records from 1715. He would die at Ocracoke with Blackbeard in their fight to the death with Captain Maynard and his men in 1718.

Archaeological Evidence

If you just got this book and skipped right to this chapter because you think you know the story you don't. Go back and read the rest of the book.

Hatteras Island is the only part of the Outer Banks that had year round inhabitants. The Croatoan lived there continuously since about the year 400. So what has been found on the soundside of Buxton and Frisco? Natives of Hatteras Island such as, Carol Dillon, Grady Austin, and Charles 'Lindy' Miller found artifacts as kids at the Croatoan Village site back in the 1930s while digging forts to play war in the woods. Charles found a large pot that was completely intact as well as several bones and arrowheads, buttons and a sword. The State of North Carolina took interest and confiscated Charles's sword. Six other people witnessed this happen and will still swear to it. There was a 1930s newspaper article by the Dare County Times about Miller's find right after he found it in 1936. The clipping of the paper was kept by Buxton native Jack Gray and given to me after an unsuccessful search of the micro film. A copy now resides at the Outer Banks history Center and in this book.

BUXTON BOY FINDS
AN ANCIENT SWORD

LINDY MILLER, young son of Mr.
and Mrs. Cantwell Miller is the
owner of an ancient sword, recently
found in a hillside near Cape Hatteras. At this spot have been
found many arrowheads, bits of
pottery and other Indian relics. At
one spot nearby, the finding of
some brass buttons led to the location of an Admiral's bones, and
they were removed by his people,
who had not known before where
he was buried. The whole section
is rich in historical significance,
and local citizens now speculate
as to what type of sword it is.
Some people think it was left there
during the Civil War.

Charles Lindy was the son of the gold medal recipi-
ent and lifesaving station keeper, Baxter B. Miller, who also
found the famous Ghost Ship. My Great-Grandfather, Estes
White, found an intact pot in the 1920s that stands a foot and
still sits on a shelf today in my Great Aunt, Mary Ormond
White Fuller's house. Almost every native of Hatteras Island

has found Indian artifacts at some point in their life. Locals have found entire Indian skeletons, bone tools, pottery, and pipes by the thousands. It is estimated that about 1500 Croatoan were living on the island in 1600.

Many of the families that currently live on the Island are descendents of the Croatoan or Hatteras Indians and some can prove it through the county records.

The problem with all archaeological finds is that the academic community rarely listens to regular people. They want an archeologist, not fishermen and children, to unearth finds. In 1938 Dr. Harrington found a 16th century English casting counter and shards of a 16th century olive jar in Buxton identical to the same objects found on Roanoke Island. In 1956, archaeologist William Haag found artifacts in the same spot as Lindy Miller's find while doing a survey of the North Carolina coast. He was the first archaeologist to record the location as the possible capital town of the Croatoan. The area of Croatoan is the entire soundside of modern day Buxton and Frisco, where a 200 acre reservation was decreed by Governor Arthur Dobbs in 1759 to the Hatteras Indians.

In 1974, another huge discovery was made on the island. An ossuary, or mass burial was uncovered in Hatteras Village. Evidence of house structures was very clear as well. The post holes stood out remarkably well in the yellow sand and an intact midden was found. In fact, the most well preserved midden in the state is on Hatteras Island. A midden is like an Indian trash pile or dump, where you can find lots of pottery sherds, shell beads, arrowheads and other items.

In 1983, archaeologist David Phelps tested the area as part of America's 400th anniversary celebration. His tests concluded that the buried stratum that contained the evidence of Croatoan Village was rich and intact.

The problem for all of the digs, despite great finds is always funding. Something needed to happen to wake North Carolina up to just what an enormously important archaeological site was sitting under Buxton and Frisco. Finally something did happen, something so horrible it is hard to be happy about it.

Hurricane Emily in 1993 was devastating to Hatteras Island. Over 25% of the people were left homeless as a result, including this author. The hurricane hit at dead high tide on a full moon. It is common knowledge on Hatteras Island that the best time to look for shipwrecks, shells, and other treasures is after a storm. This storm had top gusts of over 140mph recorded by the Buxton Coast Guard station just before a tornado caused by the hurricane ripped a splintered path through nine Coast Guard houses in Buxton. Over 10 feet of sound tide rushed over the island. Most people only had a few feet of water inside their homes, but some people literally completely lost their homes to the receding sound water, never to see their home again. The Croatoan Village site was covered with several layers of sand pushed up from the sound bottom. When this flood receded back into the sound it left the island a little surprise on the Croatoan site.

Zander Brody, a local islander, was out walking in the Croatoan area surveying the fallen trees and other damage caused by the storm when he came across an enormous amount of Native American artifacts. Zander shared his findings freely with other locals and caught the eye of a man with extreme interest. Fred Willard, a transplant from Maryland who no longer lives on the island, called religiously to state officials to get archeologists to the site. There were artifacts everywhere and it would be too big of a shame for such a discovery to go unnoticed by professionals. "Enough to fill the back of a pick-up truck," said Fred Willard about the amount of Native American artifacts and European pipes and things. Fred and local resident, Barbara Midgette donated most of the artifacts to the local museum in Frisco. The story made a local paper and not much came of it for a while.

Eventually, Fred got in touch with Dr. David Phelps. In the 1990s, Phelps began digs at Croatoan with the help of volunteers and graduate students from ECU. During these digs, Phelps found the Kendall ring and a gunlock that date back to 1583. (The ring was physically dug up by local resident and volunteer, Chris Balance). The ring is a gold signet ring that has a lion engraved on it. It was found in general debris around an Indian workshop or trading center. It probably belonged to Master Kendall, who was one of the 20 colonists sent by Ralph Lane to live on Croatoan for a month in the spring of 1586. The ring was found in 1998 and confirms the location of one of the three Croatoan villages seen on John White's maps. The gunlock was found fifty feet away from the ring in the same stratus and is identical to one in a museum back in England that was made in 1583. The ring was found in a 17th century stratus, which means that somebody kept it or wore it for a generation or two after Kendall left in 1586.

As I mentioned in the introduction, other European artifacts such as lead shot, nails, copper beads, gunflints, glass bottle fragments, coins, bale seals and bricks were found, as well as human skeletons and pig bones. (Pigs are not indigenous to America.) Much of the analysis of the archeological finds is ongoing and exciting. Many Croatoan farm tools have been found such as the whelk shell hoes used in gardens. The shells have survived and have perfectly shaped holes where the handles went in. Thomas Harriot had described these tools in a book he published in 1590 and is found in the reference page of this book. The findings do not confirm the "lost" colony went to Croatoan but do confirm the location of Croatoan and the contact with the English in 1585-86.

Who knows what else may sit below the ridges on Hatteras Island? From John White's map we see three Indian towns on the Island from Buxton to Hatteras and another area marked Paquiwoc, which means 'shallow water people' at Kinnakeet (land jetting into water). All of these villages need to be studied to learn about the Natives and possibly the abandoned colony of 1587.

More skeletons need to be found, as well as more descendents. There are two known graveyards on Hatteras Island that the locals have always called the Indian graveyards. The graves were marked by blank wooden crosses. Remember that there are no stones on Hatteras of which to make headstones out of. Most of these wooden crosses are gone now but many photographs of them exist from over the years. Where these graves came from is another mystery. So when did Croatoan Indians start marking their graves with Christian crosses? Being the oldest graveyards on the island is nothing to sneeze at. There are many graves from the 1600's. Interestingly, those graves have the names such as Payne, Harris, and Harvie, all Lost Colony surnames.

Becoming Lost

America's oldest mystery and true history needs to be told. Croatoan is where the English began their colonization, had their first feast with the Indians (Thanksgiving), and perhaps the final resting place for the Lost Colony. Why so much evidence has been ignored is strange. In the 1800's, it was widely accepted among scholars that the colony went to Croatoan and was assimilated into that tribe. It is not until 1937 that they become "lost." The Lost Colony play written by Paul Green made the colony lost forever with a romantic fiction designed to sell tickets by creating a mystery. Obviously, in 1937 the idea of 'White' people assimilating with the Croatoan or anyone who wasn't 'White' was appalling to the general audience. Therefore, facts that lead to the conclusion of assimilating are left out of the play to this day. The very idea of the colony being 'lost' is the draw of the play and the mystery is played up beyond respect. Almost nothing in the play is true. However, for some reason this is the dominant image of the colonists and the Natives. So long as people pay their hard earned money to watch this bastardization of history, the dim wits on stage will continue to fiddle and dance while shamelessly taking your money.

In addition, Ralph Lane's fort of 1585 did not go missing until after the Civil War. The Federal troops reported visiting it and even posting guards around it to keep out vandals. Within the Civil War records, there is clear indication of the fort's location if one knows how to connect the dots. There are soldiers' first hand accounts describing the earthworks of the fort of the first colony located on the

Northwest end of Roanoke Island. Many of these documents can be found online.

I personally researched the civil war records and first hand accounts that spoke of Ralph Lane's fort, and then I went to the North end of Roanoke Island, walked into the woods where the research led me and found earthworks on park service land (earthworks that they had previously been unaware of). I told the Park Service and very slowly it is being investigated. As I write this, NPS archaeologists are looking at my find. Metal detector tests have been done that I was present for along with two park rangers. There were hits all over the site. None of the hits were for zinc or lead, which is what one usually detects over civil war bullets/ sites. Most of the metal detector hits were for iron, copper, and silver. Nothing was dug up because no digging took place. This story was printed in 3 different newspapers in two states but there was never a follow up. It is possible that the earthworks are from the Civil War. There is what appears to be a 20 foot long rifle pit that everyone who has seen thinks is from the Civil War. What is strange is a series of shallow ditches that take right angles and s-curves that form a shape like a key hole or half a rectangle connected to a circle. The ditches have some square holes around them, one that is about 3 or 4 feet deep and probably 3 feet square.

After viewing the site a few months after the metal detector test, Park Service archeologists came to the site and came to no conclusions about what they saw. They never did any digging or investigation other than the walk through but the newspaper who followed them made it appear as if they had done some digging. One of the rangers, Doug Stover tripped over a log and where his hand had scraped the ground they found two musket balls. The newspaper, Outer Banks Sentinel mentioned the two musket balls as being all that was found but failed to inform the public that no actual digging took place. Hundreds of metal detector hits for items as shallow as 8 inches are left buried and unknown. You can find the original articles about the fort discovery online at the outerbankssentinel.com. The first one was titled "Fort Raleigh Found?"

So when did Ralph Lane's fort become lost? Clearly the site was well known and walked over by Civil War soldiers only 140 years ago. When did scholars and the public stop knowing where the fort was? When did they stop knowing where Croatoan was? When did the truth become lost?

I must address a major problem created by David Beers Quinn. David Beers Quinn was a very well-respected historian from Ireland, who studied the Roanoke Voyages for some 40 years, and helped with the 400th celebration of these Voyages on Roanoke Island. He also authored the book Set Fair for Roanoke: Voyages and Colonies 1584-1590. Despite his well-respected life work, this man is responsible for creating the idea that Hatteras Island could not support the colonists. Quinn seemed to think the colonists would have starved on Croatoan because the island is a poor place to farm. No where in the primary sources is this mentioned. It was simply Quinn's opinion and not a fact. What has happened is a secondary source (Quinn) has been repeated and repeated until mistakenly accepted as a fact. If anything, the primary sources suggest the soil at Croatoan in the 1580's was excellent. In Barlowe's account of 1584, he talks about the Indians yielding three separate harvests of corn a year by merely poking a hole in the ground with a stick and dropping seeds in. Barlowe was talking about Croatoan. It was at Croatoan that Barlowe tested the soil with some peas and observed that they grew 14 inches very quickly and it is Hatteras Island that Ralph Lane sent 40 of his men to live on in 1585-6 so they wouldn't starve.

We must remember that Hatteras was mush different in the 16th century than it is now. Croatoan Island in the 1580's was 20 miles long and six miles wide. In contrast, Roanoke Island was only 8 miles long and 3 miles wide, yet the English lived there for almost a year in 1585 until they ruined their relationship with the natives. The best evidence that Croatoan was an excellent place to farm comes from the Croatoan themselves. Why would they chose to live there year round for nearly 2,000 years if they could not sustain themselves? My family has farmed the land there for almost 400 years now, along with virtually every other native family on the island. The bone structure and density of the skeletons found in the Croatoan digs suggest they were either fat or muscular, at any rate the skeletons supported a large and heavy people. It is impossible to be large and heavy if you are starving. Recent studies in England suggest that people who live primarily off of meat and vegetables instead of grain are larger, which brings me to my second point.

Farming is not the only source of food. In addition to the endless supply of crabs, oysters, clams, and fish of all sorts found in the Pamlico Sound, there are deer, ducks, pheasants, and other woodland creatures all over the island. In the 1600's and 1700's, well over a thousand Europeans lived on Hatteras Island completely off the land and sea. How did Croatoan support over 1,000 immigrants a hundred years after the Lost Colony and not be able to support a mere 117 in 1587? Think about it. If the island could not support the colony then wouldn't the same hold true for the Croatoan? Why would these Indians row 35 miles across the sound to live on an island that wouldn't support them? They wouldn't. In fact they had three villages on the Island according to John White's maps. Even Quinn stated he believed over 1,000 Croatoan lived on the island in the 16th century. That is a lot of people choosing to live on a very isolated island that, according to Quinn, couldn't sustain life.

For centuries, the locals of Hatteras Island have lived off the land without any major problems. Livestock used to roam free across the island with marks behind the animals ears to let folks know who they belonged to. This was still going on well into the 1940's and there are many photographs of cows and wild horses on the beach roaming all over the island. I see no reason why the colony with the help of Manteo and his people could not survive on an island the

Croatoan had been living on successfully for nearly two-thousand years. People have always grown corn, pumpkins, cucumbers, beans and other crops on Hatteras Island. The idea that it couldn't sustain 117 extra people is ridiculous. It is also worth mentioning that Quinn was hired by the Roanoke Island Tourists Bureau, who know that the dramatic Lost Colony play is the number one tourist attraction and money maker for the island and have a financial investment in the colony staying 'lost,' an idea created and backed only by the play itself.

There is one sentence in the primary sources that supporters of Quinn will point to. When Captain Stafford first arrived at Croatoan in 1587, they asked him not to take any of their grain for they had very little. Then the document goes on to say the Croatoan invited the English to a huge feast. Tree ring data from an 800 year old cypress trees suggests that there was a severe drought in the 1587 time period for the eastern part of the state. This is probably why they had little grain that year. Besides, the drought was just as bad everywhere else across the state as well as the Chesapeake area, where Quinn thinks the colony went.

Quinn's idea that the colony went to Chesapeake comes from a report given to the Jamestown colony by Chowan Indians. This report says that the Powhatan of Roanoke killed some colonists as well as some Chesapeake Indians on Roanoke Island. Most people when they hear the word Powhatan think of Pocahontas' father. Powhatan is an Algonquin word for priest or shaman. So the Powhatan of Roanoke was not the Powhatan of the Pocahontas story. Pocahontas' father's real name was Wahunsonacok and Pocahontas' real name was Matoaka, which means clear water. There is a lake named after her on the campus of William and Mary and the mythology of Jamestown is another book for a later time. Anyway, the Powhatan of Roanoke was more than likely whoever led the Roanokes after Wingina was murdered. The account of an attack on the English at Roanoke Island by a Powhatan was more than likely referring to the one in 1586 against Grenville's 15 men.

Remember, in 1590 there was no cross carved on the tree to indicate the colony left because of danger, so we must assume they were not attacked aside from George Howe, which happened before White left. Also, remember that the Indians responsible for these two attacks had fled the area. The 1587 colonists and the Croatoan raided the fields at Dasamonquepeu and evidently the Croatoan held that area for the next 100 years, according to all the maps made in the 1600's.

We know the Roanoke Powhatan, attacked in 1586 and killed some Englishmen. So it is logical that this is the attack referred to by the Chowan Indians that informed the men at Jamestown. Also remember that 13 of Grenville's 15 men escaped the slaughter. They were last seen at an island near Port Fernando, probably modern day Cedar Island between Nags Head and Roanoke Island today (not the Cedar Island West of Ocracoke). These men could not go east, for there was nothing but ocean. They could not go west, for that was where the Indians trying to kill them were living. They could have gone south, but obviously didn't because that is Croatoan and the Croatoan reported they never saw them again. So that leaves north. The Chesapeake Indians lived just to the north. Perhaps the 13 survivors went to live with the Chesapeake. The Chesapeake were allies with the Chowan, Menatonan's people, so they may have welcomed these Englishmen, ya know after the English attacked Menatonan's village, kidnapped his son and beat him for trying to escape. So if the English survivors of the first attack made it to Chesapeake perhaps they were later killed there just as reported.

The Lost Colony went to Croatoan. We have the archaeology, genealogy, oral histories, and the primary sources to back it up. It makes the most sense of all the theories when you understand the voyages that preceded the Lost

Colony. The only argument against Croatoan is Quinn's opinion that they could not sustain themselves there.

The only real question is where did they go after they went to Croatoan? The most likely answer is that some of the colonists stayed right on Croatoan explaining why some of the Lost Colony surnames have persisted in that area and why Lawson met grey eyed Indians wearing English clothes that told him their ancestors were white people who came on Sir Walter Raleigh's ship...sigh.

Some could have migrated inland to the Coranine area, eventually being assimilated into what is now the Lumbee Tribe who still to this day claim to be Lost Colony descendants. It makes sense that over decades and centuries descendants of the Croatoan and English are found in the adjoining counties to Croatoan because people move and migrate, especially over the passing of many years.

The search for these brave settlers continues to this day. We honor them in trying to recreate their story and search for the paths that they took. It is the admiration and respect for their bravery and strength to relocate to a foreign land with the Croatoan, that drives us to want to know more about their way of life, how they survived, where they migrated to, and where they died. To keep the 'Lost Colony' a mystery on purpose, whether for financial gain or for mystique of a community, is a complete demonstration of disrespect and dishonor to those 117 courageous people who set out to start a life in a 'New World,' only to be abandoned by their mother land, have their survival skills tested to the nth degree, and survive! It is also a story of compassion and brotherhood shown by the Croatoan who accepted the burden of 117 extra mouths to feed. There exists too much evidence to say they did not pass on descendants. These hearty people survived and adapted to a new way of life. Their story lives on today, and it should be told and retold again and again.

Hatteras (Croatoan) is truly the birthplace of America, before Plymouth Rock or even Jamestown. It is the site of the first Thanksgiving or meal shared between Europeans and Native Americans, and the most logical destination of the lost (abandoned) colony. The American story began on July 4th, 1584 on an Island called.... **Croatoan**.

List of Croatoan Words

<u>Paquiwoc</u> is the oldest name we have for the village where Avon sits today. It means 'people of the shallows' pa:kwe-shallow –(w)ak is the animated plural (= people of)

<u>Kinnakeet</u> next appears on maps where in the same place as Paquiwoc and is derived from the Algonquian word Kinahkink, which means 'sharp-land-place' or 'land jetting into something' ie Pamlico Sound. The distortion of –ink into eet in English spelling is not unusual. Ahyny means 'the flats' so Kinnakeet is flat land that jets into something.

<u>Croatoan</u> is the English spelling of kurawoten pronounced (kuh-ra-woe-tain)'talking or council town. It is possible that it could be from the word kuroten which means main town or permanent town.

Micon --- food
Wutapantam --- deer
Mushaniq --- Squirrel
Nek --- My Mother
Nohsh --- My Father
Nuntanuhs --- My Daughter

Nuqisus --- My Son
Numohshomus --- My Grandfather
Nunohum --- My Grandmother
Waboose --- Rabbit
Wassador --- medal
Uppowoc --- tobacco, or to smoke
Chingwusso --- channel bass
Tesicqueo --- king snake
Crenepos --- women
Manteo --- to snatch
Wanchese --- to take flight off of water
Roanoke --- oyster money
Dasamonquepeu --- peninsula
Pamlico --- River
Win-gan-a-coa --- Welcome Friend
Ka ka torawirocs yowo --- How is this called?
Raccoon --- to scratch
Opossum --- to carry in a pouch
Winauk --- sassafras
Pagatowr --- corn
Oonossa --- pine tree
Umpe (nupuy)--- water
Wiroans --- leader, chief
Machicomuck --- temple
Kew'as --- God
Kew'asowock --- Gods
Popogusso --- Hell
Okindgier --- beans
Wickonzowr --- peas
Renapoke --- mainlander
Apis --- Sit Down
Nipatas --- Stand up

Pyas --- come here
Kurustuwes nir --- Listen to me
Kuwumaras --- I love you
Yapam --- ocean
Pumitukew --- river
Sa kir winkan? --- Are you well?
Kupi --- yes
Mahta --- no
Nuturuwins --- I am called
Ehqutonahas --- Stop Talking
Winkan nupes --- sleep well.
Chicamacomico---Place that is swept by water
Coscushaw- --greenbrier root (used to make bread)
Sapummener- --chestnut
Metaqvesvnnak ---cactus bulb
Seekanauk---horseshoe crab

These words came from Dr. Blair Rudes, Thomas
Harriot, and the Coastal Carolina Indian Center.

To see over 100 more Croatoan words and artifacts,
visit Histories and Mysteries in Buxton, NC.

Author's Note / Acknowledgments

I hope this book helps give you, the reader, some clues about the Lost Colony of 1587. I highly encourage anyone interested to pick up a copy of John Lawson's *A New Voyage to Carolina* and turn to page 45. Also try Stefan Lorant's *The New World*. That book contains all of John White's paintings as well as Barlowe, Lane, Grenville, and John White's first hand accounts. James Sprunt's: *Tales and Tradition of the Lower Cape Fear* published in 1896 has the Coree oral history reference about the missing colony on page 54. Thomas Harriot's *A Breif and True Report of the New Found Land of Virginia,* was first published in 1590 and is also a very good reference. It contains engravings based on original water colors by John White and a lot of other good information. Most of the primary sources I used in this book can be found on www.virtualjamestown.com Another great website dedicated to learning more about American Indian history and English, especially in North Carolina is www.coastalcarolindiancenter.com

When we speak of the colonists from these voyages, when we speak of 'lost' let us also remember the Croatoan and all the other tribes in this story. Their story is all that is left of a once proud, loving people who gave all they had. Their language, culture, religion, everything is lost. Millions have been spent by so many groups looking for more information on the lost colony and every detail of their lives. Our parks recreate in detail almost every trade the English had at the time from blacksmithing to dancing. Can the same be said about the American Indian history of the same time period, same story? It is a goal of mine to keep the stories alive. It is all that is left. My museum is free to all. If you want to learn about the Croatoan or the colonists come visit the island. www.thecroatoaninn.com